ARCHITECTURE
FOR ◆ THE ◆ GODS

ARCHITECTURE

FOR ◆ THE ◆ GODS

BOOK II

MICHAEL J. CROSBIE

images
Publishing

DEDICATION:

For The Reverend Hope Eakins, with much appreciation

First published in Australia in 2002 by
The Images Publishing Group Pty Ltd
ABN 89 059 734 431
6 Bastow Place, Mulgrave, Victoria, 3170, Australia
Telephone: +61 3 9561 5544 Facsimile: +61 3 9561 4860
Email: books@images.com.au
Website: www.imagespublishinggroup.com

Copyright © The Images Publishing Group Pty Ltd
The Images Publishing Group Reference Number: 440

National Library of Australia
Cataloguing-in-Publication data

Crosbie, Michael J.
Architecture for the Gods

ISBN: 1 876907 50 9 (v.II)

1. Church buildings – Pictorial works.
2. Church architecture – Pictorial works. I. Title.

726.5

Co-ordinating Editor: Robyn Beaver
Designed by The Graphic Image Studio Pty Ltd,
Mulgrave, Australia
Film by Mission Productions Limited
Printed by Everbest Printing Co. Ltd. in Hong Kong/China

IMAGES has included on its website a page for special notices in
relation to this and our other publications. Please visit this site:
www.imagespublishinggroup.com

PREFACE

A Delicate Balance

Over the past few years, an undercurrent in the architecture and design of sacred places has become a threatening rapid. In the three years since the publication of the first edition of this book, religious architectural design has begun to veer toward tradition and away from the truly experimental. This new edition of *Architecture for the Gods* is offered not only as a record of what I believe is some of the best in religious art and architecture, but also as a tonic for the constipation of creativity that seems to mark the "return to tradition" among some church architects and designers.

Religious architecture is always ripe for reactionary design. When faced with a building committee keen on "keeping the peace" within a congregation and spending funds in what they may view as a "responsible" way, it is very easy for an architect to cave in and give them the tried and true. In this case, the design process does not become an opportunity to explore the meaning of faith, the role of tradition, and the expression of a community of believers. Instead, it is architecture by rote, spiritually void and mute. As John Wesley Cook notes in his insightful Introduction to this book, religious architecture must grow from theology, and buildings that continue to repeat the forms and conventions of belief systems now defunct or in question are nothing more than empty containers.

This is not to say that architectural language with which we are familiar should be avoided. In fact, architecture (both religious and secular) often functions to help us "keep the faith." Particularly in its vernacular varieties, architecture can be an affirmation of community values, moral codes, and shared world views. But good design goes further. It not only affirms, it also challenges; in a sense, it can ask us to be clear about belief by challenging belief. Several projects in this book do just that. The Seaside Interfaith Chapel affirms the architectural values of the community at large, yet offers fresh interpretations of tradition in the use of natural light and its modulation inside. Temple Shir Tikva balances a sense of regional building tradition with an inventive response of its complex program and the need for flexibility. The Dawoodi Bohra Mosque sets down in a Dallas suburb with all of the architectural qualities to help this transplanted congregation to make a new home, yet combines traditional mosque spaces in a new way to provide privacy and shelter. None of these projects is successful by mindlessly repeating the forms and functions of the past. Instead, tradition becomes the springboard for a new way to shape space and worship.

Some projects in this book take bigger risks. They challenge the very notion of what is sacred space, and they do so in response to changing patterns of worship. Riverbend Church is one of several mega-churches in this book, and it combines a plan with an ancient precedent with accommodations for video recording and broadcast of worship. The building provides a frame for experiencing its spectacular setting, and uses nature as an inspirational backdrop within the worship space. St. Jean Vianney returns to an ancient Catholic tradition of worship in the round, yet speaks in a contemporary language that asks parishioners to look beyond the surface decoration to understand materials such as glass and stone in their spiritual dimension. For example, how the sun rakes across the surface of a poured concrete wall to reveal its making. The Sixth Church of Christ, Scientist invites us to reconsider the very nature of the storefront church and its urban presence.

Several buildings, such as the Church of Conscious Harmony and the Reno Unitarian Universalist Fellowship, meld spirituality with earth stewardship. They question our culture of consumption and its morality in a world of diminishing natural resources. Do these religious buildings express a new theology about our place on Earth and our obligations to future generations? I think they might, in beginning to ask the right questions about the nature of religious buildings and their impact on the environment.

Also present are projects that renew existing buildings by reconsidering the ritualistic use of sacred space. The renovations of the Cathedral of the Immaculate Conception and the Cathedral of St. John the Evangelist challenge the traditionalists who wish to drag the Catholic Church back to its pre-Vatican II state. This is the frontline in the architectural skirmish between reactionary and revolutionary design. The changes to St. John the Evangelist prompted a ruling from the Vatican that affirmed the new design. Other projects, such as B'Nai Jeshrun Synagogue and Emmanuel Congregation, breathe new life into old spaces, bringing the container more in line with the faith of the contained.

A final note on how this book might be used. After the first edition of *Architecture for the Gods* was published, architects told me that they had purchased several copies—one architect said he had purchased a dozen or more. I found this flattering but odd, until I understood that the book was being used as an "ice breaker" with clients. The collection of religious buildings allowed building committees, clergy, and others to consider what other possibilities there might be. Architects used the book to gauge how ready their clients might be to new ideas. In some cases it became a "wish book" for open-minded clients who felt free to speculate about their new worship space.

It is my hope that this new volume continues to fill this role. Share this book with your clients, pore over its pages, consider how congregations small and large, rich and poor have found ways to design and build houses of God and homes for worship. Learn from those who have gone before, and begin a new journey.

Michael J. Crosbie

CONTENTS

Architecture for the Gods Book II

INTRODUCTION

In the Search

From the evidence that is presented in the excellent photographs and descriptive material in this book, it is clear that among new church buildings, there are many that introduce new styles and variations on old styles. Partially because the practice of church architecture is represented by many firms in cooperation with varied congregations in different parts of the country, there is little commonality that emerges from these examples. This is a good thing because it signals, among other things, that church architecture is going through a stage of experimentation, change, and a search for adequate forms. The collection here is solid evidence that such a search is underway.

The times demand that the search be undertaken, and that adequate forms be given. The past is full of good examples of successful attempts at church architecture. There are at least two examples that still shape the present: the Neo-Gothic style and the Colonial style. Both are popular among present congregations, and they are the styles most often mentioned as "ideal" when architects, at the beginning of a project, ask congregations what a church building should look like. Such answers very often provide architects with an easy way out, and contribute to what has become a mundane and destructive way of doing church architecture. There is an unfortunate trend, even today, that repeats the Neo-Gothic and Colonial styles. Unfortunate because the meanings that gave rise to those styles have been lost but nevertheless, the forms remain and are constantly repeated.

For instance, when the "Gothic" was invented, there was a belief in the efficaciousness of the sacrament as it was taken (in one species) in medieval liturgical practice. At the same time, there was the use of proportions and stained glass in their architecture that had sacramental value. The invention to which I refer is a serious initiative that grew out of the relationship with the theological leaders of the day and their understanding of the way materials, especially in architectural practice, were used. That is to say, the so-called "Gothic" result was theologically motivated. It is strongly believed, based on the most recent scholarship, that the earliest realization of the Gothic solution came under the direct influence of Abbot Suger at St. Denis near Paris, France. Abbot Suger had traveled widely and knew well what the artisans of the day could accomplish. He led them, during the tedious process of putting the church building of St. Denis together, to implement his theological perspective. There was a liturgical preference that Suger articulated and which brought about the forms that we see today. The artists and architects of the 12th century did not always understand what they were accomplishing, but they did know that they were serving a deeply Christian agenda for building and decorating. The forms were so strong and important at the time that they became fixtures in the Christian imagination and subsequently became a popular idiom for municipal, collegiate, and private architecture. Today the original 12th- and 13th-century Gothic meanings are gone but the forms linger on. For the 21st century, Gothic and Neo-Gothic church buildings represent dead forms that continue because of nostalgia and associations with the past.

Some of the same can be said about the constant repetition of Colonial forms of architecture. It was Christopher Wren, after the fire in London of 1666, who introduced a church architecture that paid close attention to the word preached and the adequate hearing of the same. Wren designed a series of church buildings that arranged the listeners within a good hearing distance from the preacher. Even his earliest design for St. Paul's, London followed that theology. The clerics at St. Paul's prevented that structure from being built, but Wren's idea is preserved in a wooden model that can be studied in the basement display in St. Paul's today. It is a matter of record that his architecture had a strong influence on early-American church buildings. "Copy books" that included his plans and steeple designs were well known. It is clear in those early American sacred spaces that some architectural details were introduced to serve worship practices exclusively. For instance, in some early church buildings the pulpit was raised up about halfway between the congregation on the first floor and the balconies (or galleries) where part of the congregation sat on the second level. This design motif, which was followed throughout 17th- and 18th-century Christian church building, was acoustically sensitive. The elevated place of the preacher in the pulpit was designed for the preacher to be seen and well heard. Also, there is an alteration in the fenestration in those old meetinghouse buildings. When the pulpit was placed on the side of the short axis of the building, a window was placed behind the preacher, half way up the wall and in the middle of the exterior elevation of the windows. When I first studied these buildings I thought it an odd motif, and it had been repeated in many examples. Among other things, it put light behind the speaker and made it difficult for the congregation to see him or her. At least, I thought it odd until I actually stood in one of the pulpits in question and it became quite clear. The window behind the pulpit was placed there primarily for the preacher's benefit. The preacher normally preached during midday and the light assisted the reading of scripture and his notes for sermon. Therefore, the odd position of the window was determined by the importance of the scripture and the sermon in worship. Although the Colonial style (here meaning the period from early American meetinghouse designs through the Federal period of church architecture) became popular because it was based on a theology of the preached word, the repetitions that continue to appear to this day seem to have copied a form rather than the original meanings that gave shape to that form. Those church buildings, when produced as new church architecture in the 21st century, seem to be the products of nostalgia and association with the past—not a living architecture.

We are beyond the practice of continuing to repeat dead forms in architecture if the evidence given here by Michael Crosbie is taken seriously. This collection, when studied carefully, will illustrate that we have moved beyond easy solutions to the imaginative state of being "in the search" for adequate buildings to house our best contemporary values for worship and the ongoing life of the spirit. Can we say that we know where church architecture is going? Is there a dominant form in which we can see the shape of the future for sacred spaces? There seem to be three directions now. One is that mentioned above—namely, that nostalgia is, unfortunately, shaping the future.

Second, there is the new phenomenon of the so-called "mega-churches," several of which are represented in this book. These very large structures are dotting the American landscape, as huge congregations are attracted to newer modes of technological and artistic expression. These forms follow a cultural phenomenon. They accommodate a large number of people who are placed in comfortable theater chairs in very large amphitheater-shaped "sanctuaries." The large audience makes the participant an observer and the worship leaders more like entertainers. When I have visited mega-

churches during their worship services, the forms of worship, as well as the architecture, reflect more a shopping mall environment, and popular art forms in the music and literature predominate. The role of technology is very important in these new spaces. Often monitors on the walls show what is happening on the "stage." Traditional symbols of the Christian faith are obscure or totally absent, vestments are avoided, and an atmosphere is created that seems to be more like an audience at an entertainment event than a traditional congregation at worship. These forms are very imposing and important now in American church architecture. Seldom is a particular architect cited as the planner or designer of a mega-church.

The third important influence on the architecture of sacred spaces is the creative use of new materials and new methods of construction that give life, experimentation, and flexibility to planning. It is clear that the place of glass in new planning has increased the use of illumination and structural innovation. Modern uses of concrete have given architects new possibilities for worship environments. Technologies, in many modalities, have been incorporated by architects in ways that have enhanced the worship experience. There are positive innovations that have been introduced by creative architects to congregations that are asking for contemporary forms that work for their purposes.

In the present world of the construction of sacred spaces, there is less leadership on the part of clergy than is needed. Too often the congregation's response is given by self-selected members who provide easy answers. The clergy are not prepared to take seriously the language of architecture for the purposes of the church's mission, and too often the architect is left to make decisions that should be mutually shared.

In the midst of this transitional period there are many good solutions in the search for modern homes for worshipping communities. These examples, some of which are recorded in this book, are messages for the future of those who want meaningful, spiritual spaces. These houses of worship constitute a new spirit that is expressed by clergy, congregations, and architects working together to bring vitality, meaning, and beauty to the ultimately important business of housing the practices of believing communities before a living God.

John Wesley Cook

PROJECTS

CHAPEL OF THE APOSTLES

Maurice Jennings + David McKee Architects

The Chapel of the Apostles at the University of the South in Sewanee, Tennessee serves both as a place of worship and as a classroom where School of Theology students practice the rituals of worship in the Episcopal Church. The 8500-square-foot chapel seats 250 people and its towering form defines the presence of the School of Theology on the campus. The chapel is a spiritually uplifting space, connected with the campus yet sheltering and internally focused, designed according to the principles of organic architecture as espoused by Frank Lloyd Wright and by Fay Jones. These principles include a harmony between the building and its natural surroundings, a close relationship of the individual elements of a building to each other, carefully controlled natural light, and the honest use of materials.

Low native sandstone walls extend from the chapel, anchoring it to the land. The native flagstone floor of the forecourt continues uninterrupted into the narthex, blurring the division between outside and inside and providing a feeling of harmony between the building and its site. The wood mullion pattern that subdivides the entry glass announces a recurring geometric theme in the custom-built bronze entry door pulls, interior and exterior lights, furnishings, and items used in services. The low ceiling beneath the organ loft, which separates the narthex and sanctuary, compresses the space and dramatizes the emergence into the 48-foot-tall sanctuary.

Continued

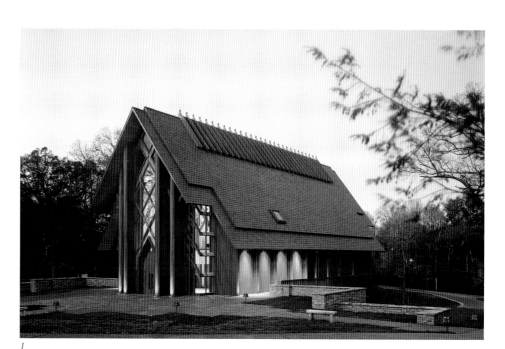

1

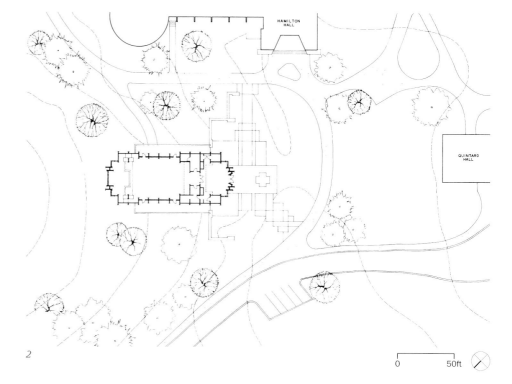

1   View of chapel from west
2   Site plan
3   Main entrance to chapel

2

0   50ft

3

Overhead, wood structural members bound together with custom architectural metal gussets and brackets create structural "bents" that direct the worshipper's eyes reverently skyward.

The generously glazed walls and large ridge skylights permit a pattern of light and shadow, continually changing with the time of day and passage of seasons, to bathe the walls, floors, and structural members. Natural light from skylights also illuminates the sacristy and enlivens the small oratory chapel. A simple palette of stone, glass, steel, and wood, and judicious use of muted colors serve both to unify the composition and further relate the building to its environment.

4

5

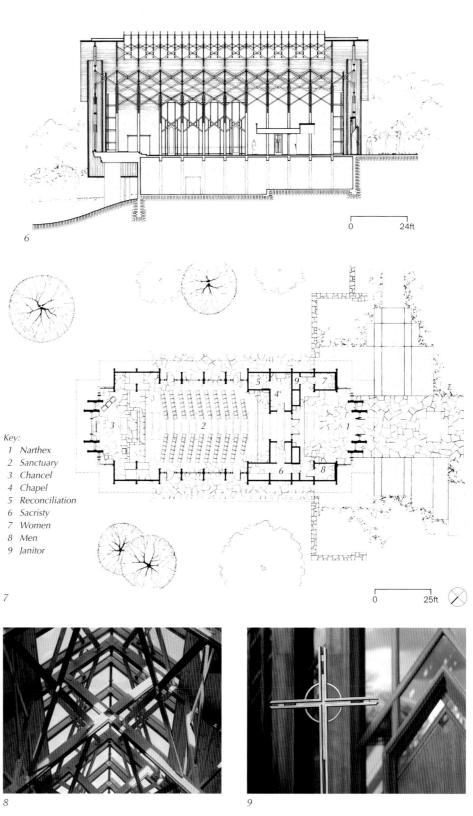

6

Key:
1 Narthex
2 Sanctuary
3 Chancel
4 Chapel
5 Reconciliation
6 Sacristy
7 Women
8 Men
9 Janitor

7

0   24ft

0   25ft

8

9

4 *East elevation is dominated by sheltering roof*
5 *View toward altar from entrance*
6 *Section*
7 *Floor plan*
8 *Detail of intricate roof structure*
9 *Detail of cross design*
Photography: Richard Johnson

B'NAI JESHURUN SYNAGOGUE

Bromley Caldari Architects

The present home of Congregation B'nai Jeshurun in New York, New York was built in 1917. The exterior is a stark composition of granite relieved by a highly decorated portal with a stained glass rose window. The interior is highly decorated, with Moorish motifs rendered in a polychrome of gold, red, teal blue, and forest green. A significant and much-loved feature of the building was its stalactite-festooned jute plaster ceiling.

Under the leadership of the late Rabbi Marshall Meyer, a project to restore the building was undertaken and during the course of that work a portion of the ceiling collapsed and the project was abandoned. In 1995 the congregation initiated a modest restoration/renovation project.

With the growth of the congregation, it was noted that the old sanctuary's traditional sloping floor would no longer accommodate the music and dance orientation of the liturgy nor the

spatial requirements of the community. In addition to weekly services, the restored sanctuary was to be used for classes, weddings and Bar-Mitzvahs, dinners, performances, children's activities in association with a neighboring school, and committee meetings.

Estimates for repairing and restoring the ceiling exceeded US$1 million—a prohibitive amount. The architect's response was rational yet inspirational.

Continued

1

2

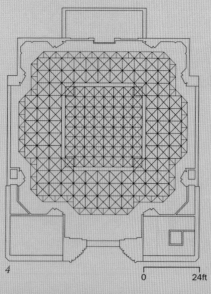

1   Front façade of synagogue
2   Entry hall
3   Space frame hovers over worship space
4   Space frame plan
5   Movable seats allow for maximum flexibility

3

4

0   24ft

5

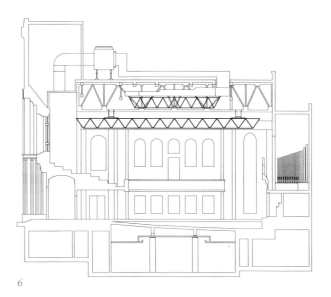

6

After designing a support grid based on panel points of the roof trusses, what followed logically was a solution that would span between points in both directions and require minimal support over the long span central section—in short, a space frame. The frame is floated away from the existing walls, placing it within the envelope of the sanctuary as an independent element meant to contrast yet complement the existing polychrome and stained glass. The space frame also allows access to the highly flexible lighting system via a catwalk on the top chord. HVAC ducts are directly above the frame and acoustic treatments are applied directly to the underside of the roof slab.

The renovation, restoration, and alterations to the building along with the restoration work were carried out under Rabbi Meyer's edict "to look forward as we embrace the past."

6   Section
7   Overview of restored worship space
Opposite:
    Detail of restored arc and bema
Photography: Peter Mauss/Esto

7

RIVERBEND CHURCH

Overland Partners

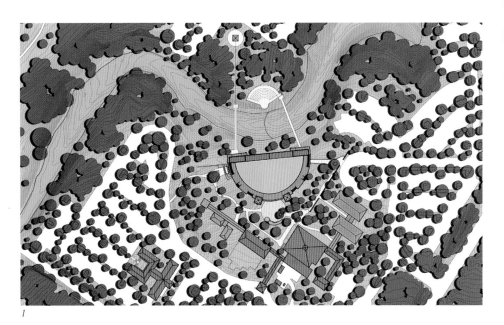

1

This new, hill-country sanctuary serves a growing contemporary Christian community in Austin, Texas with unusual programmatic needs. Drawing inspiration from classical stone amphitheaters, the sanctuary is positioned at the edge of a steep precipice. The amphitheater form meets the congregation's objective that the sanctuary be conducive to welcoming people uninspired by traditional worship environments. The design of the seating ensures that no congregant is more than 90 feet from the altar, and creates a visually dynamic interior space in dialogue with the exterior terrain. Framed through a large arched window is a view of the adjacent deep ravine, creating a beautiful backdrop for spiritual celebrations and drama.

The spectacular natural setting is the genesis for an earthy palette of warm materials, including wood, limestone, sandstone, and painted metal, used throughout the sanctuary. At the entry, massive limestone monoliths anchor two masonry and glass towers that act as beacons within the landscape. The symbolic broad arch, articulated in limestone, sandstone, and wood at the entry and repeated in the backdrop to the altar, recalls a rainbow seen following a storm at the first major on-site event. The sighting gave rise to the symbolic term for the community as a "home for hope" for the disenfranchised.

Versatility in the design of the sanctuary, with full television broadcast and production facilities plus state-of-the-art theatrical and performance technology, allows it to accommodate worship and theatrical performances by the congregation, as well as public concerts and local symphony performances. The sanctuary is also enriched by the work of local craftspeople and artists. At the entry, a terracotta crown of thorns is centered in a recess among a dozen windows, as an abstract representation of Christ and the 12 apostles. The congregation set aside one percent of its building fund to commission additional works of art for the sanctuary over time. In the narthex, a local artist has completed a 40-foot-long fresco, one of the largest created in this region, depicting the return of the Prodigal Son.

2

3

4

1 Site plan
2 Approach to church from pathways
3 Gentle arch marks entrance to church
4 View of church from across the river

5   *View up into light-filled stair tower*
6   *Glass-enclosed stair tower overlooks countryside*
7   *Main entry level floor plan*
8   *Overview of sanctuary, with views beyond*

5

6

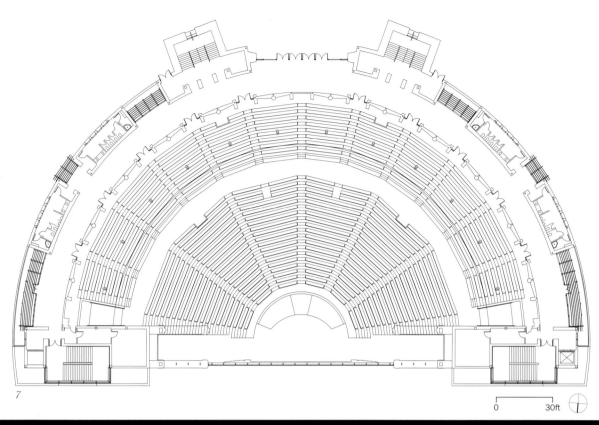

7

0   30ft

8

Opposite:
Raked seating in a semicircle around stage
10   *Sanctuary space filled to capacity*
11   *Video screen is used during services*
Photograpy: Paul Bardagjy (3-5,8-10);
Patrick Wong (2,6,11)

10

11

CATHEDRAL OF THE IMMACULATE CONCEPTION RESTORATION

Williamson Pounders Architects

In response to the needs of a vital parish and the expanding Catholic Diocese of Memphis, Williamson Pounders Architects designed the restoration of the Cathedral of The Immaculate Conception in Memphis, Tennessee through the implementation of a two-phase, twelve-year master plan. Fr. Richard Vosko was the liturgical consultant.

The restoration brings the cathedral into full conformance with contemporary Roman Catholic liturgical standards. The redesign of the main front entrance provided new curving front steps, a broad paved plaza, and new lighting and landscaping. The window-lined stair gallery addition links the basement with the main worship space. At its top is located the new marble tomb for the first bishop of the diocese, a major benefactor of the cathedral. A new

amphitheater is found immediately outside the structure to allow access and natural light to the new basement fellowship hall. A kitchen, restrooms, offices, classrooms, choir rehearsal room, and sacristy were also provided.

In the main worship space the altar table was moved forward into the center of the nave on a raised platform and surrounded by new pews and movable chairs. A new marble baptismal font, incorporating the old altar railing and the old font, was added near the main entrance. Old acoustical tiles were removed and the central dome was rebuilt to improve acoustics. The newly unified decorative motif includes both new and restored murals, while the vaulted ceiling was decorated with 23-carat gold-leaf stars. The Stations of the Cross were renovated, stained glass windows were restored, and the

old flooring was replaced by a red oak floor with inlaid patterns. The balcony was reconfigured to provide additional seating.

The east transept was reconfigured for an expanded choir and future pipe organ. The west transept features a new skylit Blessed Sacrament Chapel, Reconciliation Chapel, and two-story entry vestibule. Elevators and ramps were added to make the cathedral completely accessible. All new computer-controlled lighting and sound reinforcement systems were provided.

The architects also designed the new liturgical furnishings, including the altar table, celebrants' chairs and cathedra, pulpit, oils ambry, tabernacle stand, processional cross, and candleholders.

1

2

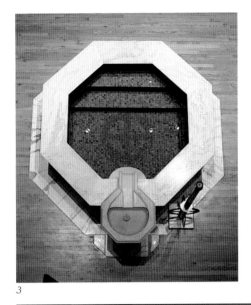

3

4

1 Front façade illuminated to dramatize approach from entry plaza
2 Altar table repositioned on raised platform near center of congregation
3 New font seen from above
4 New processional cross has removable corpus
5 New stair gallery opens access to basement spaces
6 Floor plan
7 Blessed Sacrament chapel features gold-leafed dome

Photography: James F. Williamson, FAIA (1,2,3,6); Mim Studios (5); Jeffrey Jacobs (4,7)

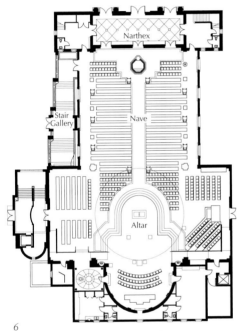

6

5

7

PRAIRIE REPOSE CEMETERY CHAPEL

Saavedra Gehlhausen Architects

Members of the Eckburg family sought to renovate this cemetery chapel in Amboy, Illinois as a gift in memory of their parents. Their objective was to bring this dormant, unused building back to life. The 645-square-foot chapel, built in 1905, had not been used for nearly 30 years and was occupied only by birds and other wildlife that found refuge through the broken stained glass windows.

The chapel's exterior stone was cleaned and restored. The stained glass was restored and rebuilt, and protective glazing was added to the exterior. A landscaped entry plaza was added, providing accessibility for the disabled and an outside space for people to gather before and after services.

Design of the floor plan and interior layout was to provide flexibility for various worship and secular functions. This goal was achieved by utilizing custom-designed, movable pews and liturgical furnishings. The chapel's interior features painted wood paneling, newly restored stained glass windows, and a new ceramic floor in a checkered pattern—all in keeping with the chapel's original architectural style. The light colors used on the interior lift the spirits and provide a contemplative atmosphere for the remembrance of loved ones and celebration of their lives.

The chapel is now alive at Prairie Repose Cemetery after more than a generation of abandonment. It is enjoying a second life as a setting for Bible studies, string quartet concerts, and weddings, as well as memorial services.

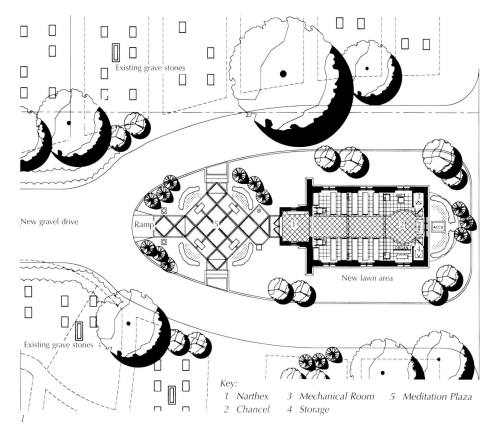

Existing grave stones

New gravel drive

Ramp

New lawn area

Existing grave stones

Key:
1 Narthex   3 Mechanical Room   5 Meditation Plaza
2 Chancel   4 Storage

1

2

3   Restored interior with view toward entry
4   Light colors and uplighting lift the
    chapel interior
Photography: McGinty Photography

3

4

TEMPLE SHIR TIKVA

Solomon + Bauer Architects

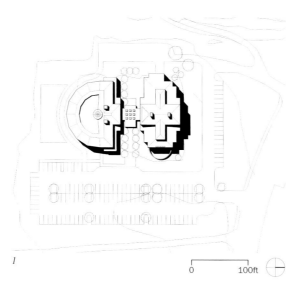

1

0   100ft

Located on busy Route 20 in Wayland, Massachusetts, this project combines worship space with facilities needed for education, geared to a growing congregation. The complex takes the form of two wings: one housing the sanctuary, social hall, and foyer; the other containing a reception area, a chapel/meeting room, classrooms, and administrative offices. A one-story skylit entrance lobby connects the two.

The sanctuary wing meets the need for flexibility through its design, and offers the option for three totally separate spaces: a sanctuary seating 200, a social hall seating 150, and a foyer seating 100. It is also possible to combine the three spaces to accommodate the entire congregation on high holy days or to use the foyer as needed to enlarge either the sanctuary or social hall. The ark, reader's desk, and candle tables in the sanctuary were designed by the architect and fabricated from cherry wood.

The 26,500-square-foot education wing is centered around a two-story skylit central living area. On the first floor are five nursery school classrooms, a chapel/meeting room, a reception area, and the temple administrative center. The nursery school classrooms can be converted to religious school classrooms using a custom-designed pivoting wall system. The wall system accommodates either large open nursery school classrooms or smaller religious school classrooms with generous closet areas for storage of nursery school equipment. The curved form of the classrooms surrounds an exterior play yard for the nursery school.

On the second floor are eight religious school classrooms, a school library, and private offices. The generous corridor space, which is designed to accommodate students waiting between classes, overlooks the central living area below.

Designed to complement its New England village surroundings, the white-painted wood trim and clapboard structure uses generous glass areas and clerestories to maximize the infusion of light to interior spaces and to insulate the congregation from the sights and sounds of the busy thoroughfare. Glass doors lead to a memorial garden off the sanctuary and to a courtyard off the lobby, between the social hall and chapel/meeting room.

2

1 Site plan
2 Classroom/administration wing to the left, sanctuary to the right
3 Section

3

4   View of sanctuary wing from the north
5   Sanctuary with soft light from above
6   First floor plan
7   Living room is naturally lit from roof monitor
Photography: Steve Rosenthal

4

5

Key:
1 Lobby   9 Office
2 Foyer   10 Coats
3 Sanctuary   11 Conference
4 Social hall   12 Copy
5 Memorial garden   13 Chapel/meeting room
6 Kitchen   14 Convertible nursery school classroom
7 Living room   15 Nursery school classroom
8 Administration

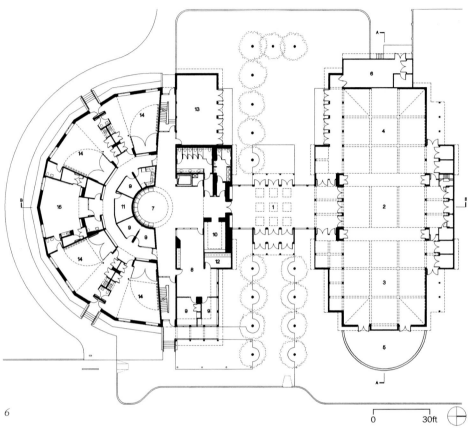

6

0   30ft

7

RENO UNITARIAN UNIVERSALIST FELLOWSHIP

Pfau Architecture

The Unitarian Universalist Fellowship of Northern Nevada has a striking and sustainable new fellowship hall. The US$1.4 million project includes a 3000-square-foot Great Room at the heart of the building, meeting rooms, offices, and an entrance gathering space. The facility serves a growing, 250-person congregation in Reno, Nevada.

The congregation expressed interest in a sustainable, enduring, low-maintenance facility that would be closely connected to the surrounding natural environment. The site is buffered to the south by land slated for wetlands park development and boasts spectacular views of the Sierra Nevada mountain range to the south and west.

The design approach sought to express the "spirituality of materiality." Simple, elegant forms are rendered in tactile, healthy materials that are unaltered from their natural state, including high fly-ash concrete block, wood, poured concrete, cement board siding, and metal. Wood structural members are exposed and consist of large glulam roof trusses and clean-peeled tree columns.

The 24-foot-high Great Room is a glazed pavilion that is visually connected to the landscape. Louvered shading devices optimize seasonal passive solar performance, allowing heat gain in the winter and shading in the summer while preserving mountain views. The glazed walls admit large amounts of natural light, virtually eliminating the need for artificial lighting.

Continued

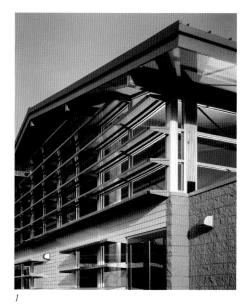

1

Key:
1 Existing building—religious education
2 Day care
3 Entry ramp
4 Gathering room
5 Great Room
6 Office
7 Office
8 Office
9 Library

2

0   40ft

1 Louvers on wall allow sun to be shaded
2 Site plan
3 Front entrance to building is understated yet welcoming
4 Great Room glows with warmth

3

4

5   Section
6   Great Room is a column-free space with
     natural light
7   Entry into lobby and Great Room beyond
Opposite:
     Light from glazed walls can be modulated
     with louvers
Photography: Cesar Rubio

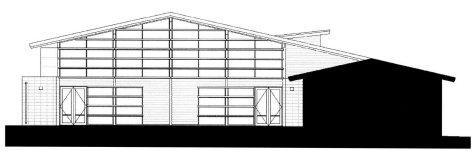

5

6

The siting, building masses, and building
systems are organized with the goal of minimal
intervention with the landscape. An advanced
hydronic mechanical system requires very little
energy to maintain an even temperature.
Radiant heating in the concrete floor slab is
delivered by tubes filled with water, which is
stored in a 10,000-gallon reservoir on the west
side of the building. In the Great Room, a
supplemental fan-coil system, fed by heated and
cooled tubes, works in conjunction with the
ventilation. The exposed concrete floor slab, the
earth below the slab, and the reservoir provide
the thermal mass to keep temperatures steady;
baseline floor temperatures are 59°F in winter
and 69°F in summer.

7

VIENNA PRESBYTERIAN CHURCH

LeMay Erickson Architects

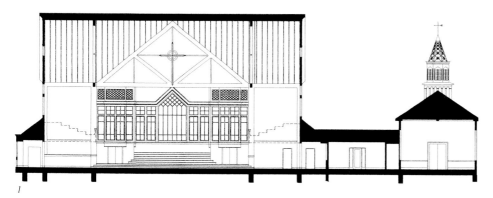

1

This church, the largest Presbyterian congregation in Virginia, has occupied its current location in Vienna since construction of its first church building in 1874. Today, the immediate context of the church retains much of its original semi-rural character and scale, with historical, white frame buildings fronting a large open "village green." Because of the congregation's veneration of its historic chapel and a commitment to remain at this site, sensitive engagement of the chapel and adjoining vernacular architecture was essential in the design of a new 750-seat sanctuary.

Working with building forms and detailing suggested by the context, the new sanctuary takes the form of a Greek cross in plan. Within each arm of the cross plan, balconies create an intimate and dynamic sense of worship gathering despite the large seating capacity. The cross plan is revealed on the exterior in gabled roofs that help blend the new structure with the diminutive scale of adjacent historic structures.

The new building is sheathed in western red cedar board-and-batten siding, emphasizing the vertical character of the new addition, and

reducing its apparent mass. Aluminum tube grillwork in the new chancel pediment and entry porticoes recalls the adjacent 1874 chapel cupola. The entire assemblage is placed on a unifying brick base, visually reducing the building mass, linking new and old worship spaces, and providing an appropriate institutional presence.

Inside the sanctuary, the wood batten theme is applied to the large ceiling planes, providing subtle visual texture and acoustical reinforcement for the church's pipe organ. A 14-foot-tall cross commands the space from its central position on the large truss above the chancel. Simple, natural red oak accents at door and window heads provide understated, elegant detailing. Large operable oak shutters further enhance the visual warmth while allowing the room to be darkened for special occasions.

In both form and detail, the new church is firmly grounded in the Presbyterian "meeting house" heritage while providing a contemporary home for this large congregation's diverse ministry needs.

1   West section
2   1874 chapel and new sanctuary

2

3

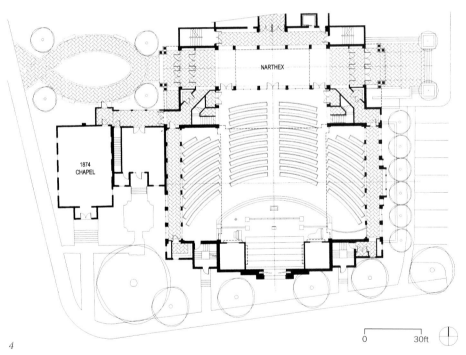

NARTHEX

1874
CHAPEL

0   30ft

4

3 Exterior of new church, with older building
   visible at left
4 First floor plan
5 View into chancel from narthex
Photography: Dan Cunningham

5

THE POTTER'S HOUSE

The Beck Group

Within two years of the establishment of the Potter's House in an existing church in Dallas, Texas the weekend attendance exceeded 10,000 people. The congregation was ready for a new sanctuary to be built adjacent to the existing building. The new building seats 8200 and provides full broadcast capabilities. The exterior form of the building was shaped by the need to complete construction in a very short period of time. The simple box shape, combined with the structural concrete tilt walls, allowed for a very fast erection time. The design emphasized the planar nature of these concrete panels. A series of floating concrete planes defines the lobby area as well as the tower. Because of remote parking locations many worshippers are transported by shuttle bus; a large metal canopy provides enough cover for three buses to unload simultaneously.

The core of the worship service is the preaching of Bishop T.D. Jakes and the interaction that takes place between him and the congregation. The seating wraps around the platform, providing the bishop the sense of being in the audience, and allows the congregation to see each other reacting to his powerful preaching style.

A balcony was used to tighten the space and reduce the distance to the back wall. By allowing this balcony to flow down to the main level on either side of the platform, the sense of separation between the two levels is minimized.

As a broadcast television studio, the sanctuary accommodates lighting, mechanical, and sound elements in the ceiling. However, the client wanted a finished ceiling that would hide all of these elements. A series of "clouds" was designed to fit around the multiple rows of catwalks. These curved screens allow the catwalks an unobstructed view to the stage, while providing a finished surface when viewed from the audience. The undulating "clouds" add a depth to the ceiling and can be lit to vary the mood in the space. The "cloud" closest to the stage is made of sound-transparent fabric to accommodate the major speaker clusters.

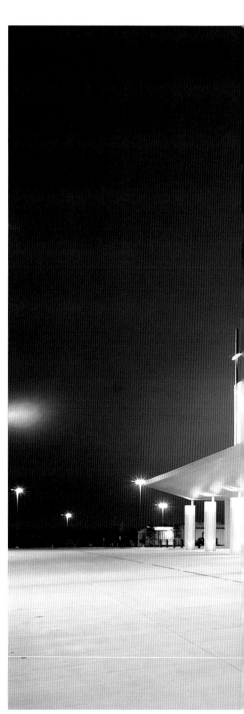

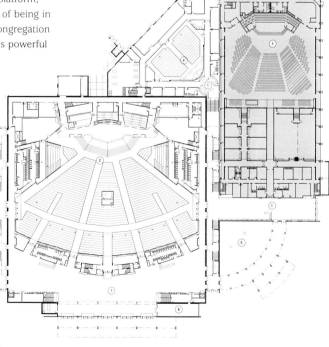

Key:
1   Lobby
2   Sanctuary
3   Existing building
4   Chapel
5   Baptistry and garden
6   Bookstore
7   Sanctuary balcony level

1

1   First floor plan
2   Detail of cross at entry
Below:
    Overview of building as it greets visitors

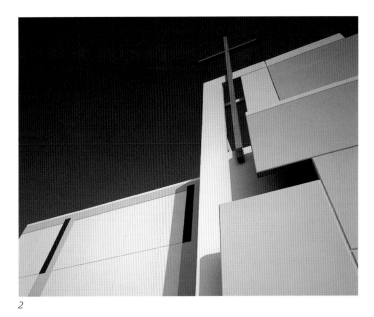
2

4

4   Interior focuses on worship stage area
5   Sanctuary from under a balcony
6   Worship space in use
7   Entry to sanctuary
Photography: Mark Trew

5

6

7

CONGREGATION MICAH

Michael Landau Associates

1

2

3

This new 29,500-square-foot Reform synagogue is in the foothills of Nashville, Tennessee's rolling mountains. The building is set back on its 38-acre site, closer to the hills beyond, and establishes the natural setting by preserving 24 acres of protected wetlands. The approach to the synagogue is orchestrated through the trees and flowering meadow. Drawing inspiration from the walls of Jerusalem, yellow-gold bricks are layered in patterns that resemble the large cut stone and varied patterns of the ancient temple's Western Wall. Worshippers are drawn through the entry and into a traditionally inspired Jewish community.

In the new building the openness of the corridors is reminiscent of an ancient *shtetl*, but without the dark and narrow feel of the old world. The sanctuary is a deliberate departure from the enclosed and sheltered synagogues of the *shtetl*. It is welcoming, airy, and filled with the light of the open countryside. The room seats 300 in just seven rows, with remarkable intimacy. Panels along the sanctuary's curved rear wall open to accommodate 1200 for the high holy days.

At the center of this space, the Torah scrolls are sheltered in a cylindrical ark that is at the heart of the building, forming the base for the seven steel trusses that spring to support the roof like the branches of a menorah or the tree of life. Designed by Michael Berkowicz, Ori Resheff, and Bonnie Srolovitz of Presentations Gallery, the curved copper doors of the ark are inscribed with the Ten Commandments. Beneath the base of the ark, the written prayers of the adults and children—their hopes and dreams for the future—are sealed in the concrete floor.

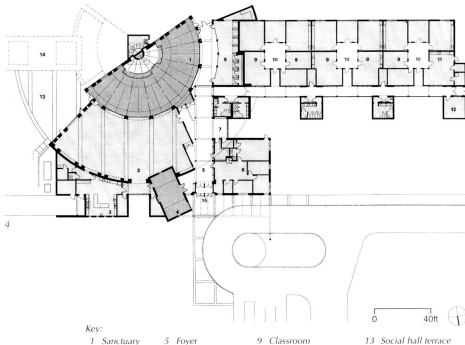

4

1 View of exterior from northwest
2 South elevation of sanctuary wing
3 Trusses arch over the worship space
4 Floor plan
Opposite:
   Ten Commandments are cut into the
   ark's copper doors
Photography: William Lafevor

Key:
1 Sanctuary	5 Foyer	9 Classroom
2 Social hall	6 Administration	10 Common area
3 Kitchen	7 Gift shop	11 Youth lounge
4 Chapel	8 Library	12 Educational support

13 Social hall terrace
14 Future ampitheater
   and sculpture garden
15 Entrance

0   40ft

St. Peter the Apostle Catholic Church

Davis Durand-Hollis Rupe Architects

1

2

3

The design intentions for the sanctuary addition at St. Peter the Apostle in Bourne, Texas are rooted in the liturgical rituals and the strong influence of the architecture of the existing 1923 church building. Worship space that embraces the people and recognizes the diversity of cultures shared within the community was the primary design criteria.

Project requirements for the new sanctuary called for a master plan that "cleaned up" a site with multiple buildings in various stages of repair. The six-acre site is divided into three parts because of the property's extreme slope. Several existing structures were demolished to allow for circulation and exterior gathering before and after services.

The exterior walls of light-colored stone act as a canvas for the earlier church. The towers of the original church remain the focus from Main Street—a desired result expressed by the community.

An antiphonal plan allows for seating of 850 worshippers in an intimate setting. The baptismal font with overflowing water welcomes one into the nave. The interior foyer allows for a continuous procession from the outdoor gathering space through the large entry, to the font, ambo, and altar. The main focus is the altar, raised on a platform and embraced by the assembly. The truss forms emphasize the large open ritual area. Skylights and large windows allow for light to spill onto the walls and floors, lighting the natural materials of stone, wood, and brick. Windows and glass connect nature with the interior space. The elements of water, earth (stone), and sky are celebrated here as God's gifts to his people.

The forms are a reflection of the materials used in the original church. Natural, hand-hewn materials help forge a link between the new space and the church's past. Ornamentation is simple and integrated with the architecture.

1 Protected entry to narthex
2 Stairs leading to plaza at church front
3 View along wall of existing church, as new wing steps out
4 Floor plan
5 Stations of the Cross at sanctuary periphery
6 View of the sanctuary from font to chancel
7 Font near entrance to sanctuary
8 New chapel inside renovated church
Photography: Larry Pearlstone

Key:
1 Narthex   7 Chapel   13 Reconciliation
2 Font   8 Nursery   14 Day chapel
3 Sanctuary   9 Usher's room   15 Pipes
4 Altar   10 Chapel   16 Piano
5 Choir area 11 Vestibule   17 Organ
6 Sacristy   12 Reservation

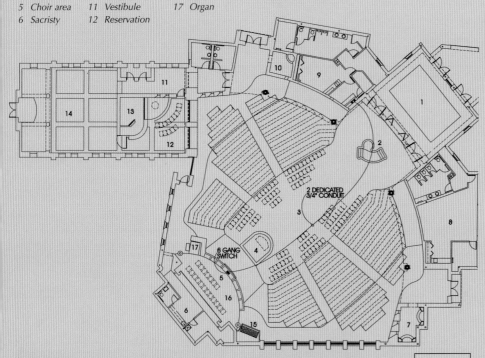

4

5

6

7

8

CHICAGO CULTURE CENTER

Harding Associates

1

The Chicago Culture Center is a Buddhist Temple and Midwest headquarters for Soka Gakkai International, the largest religious society in Japan. The 28,000-square-foot Chicago Culture Center consists of three auditoriums with capacities of 600, 150, and 50 seats respectively, an exhibition gallery, executive offices, training rooms, and a bookstore. The siting of the center continues the Chicago tradition of major buildings terminating streets. The main lobby is centered on the axis of 14th Place at Wabash. Building forms are drawn from Chicago architectural traditions.

Use of building interstitial spaces by structural, mechanical, electrical, and plumbing systems was thoroughly designed and coordinated. The design team utilized strategies that had been applied to systems integration in high-rise buildings in order to maximize available interior space and minimize the height of the interstitial zone.

Major materials and building systems were researched and value-engineered to provide a durable and cost-effective solution, while meeting the stringent functional criteria of the client. Materials also reflect the heritage of Chicago architecture. Early in the design process, the compact, dense massing of the building was determined to provide the most cost-effective approach. The design was broken down into primal shapes that reflected the internal functional arrangement and yielded an appealing scale to an otherwise large building. Glazing was carefully clustered to provide views of the Chicago skyline from the offices and to open up the main lobby at the termination of the 14th Place axis on Wabash. In order to economize, other elevations have minimal glazing.

2

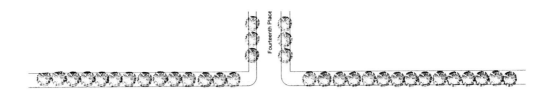

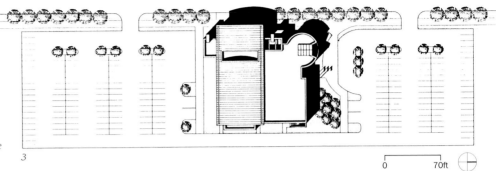

1   Vehicular approach to building
2   Detail of west elevation
3   Site plan
4   Materials are inspired by Chicago architecture

3

0   70ft

4

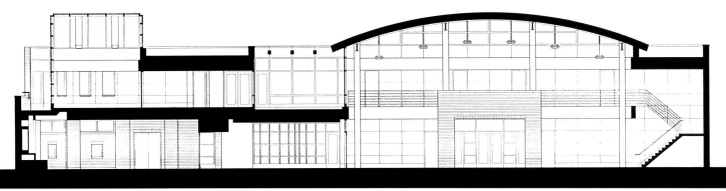

5

6

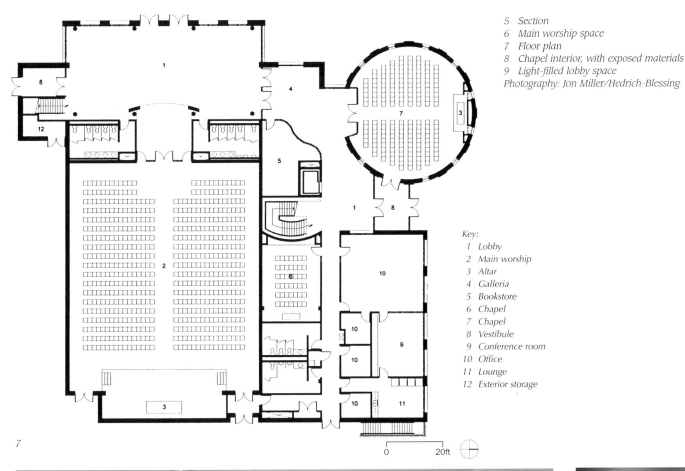

5   Section
6   Main worship space
7   Floor plan
8   Chapel interior, with exposed materials
9   Light-filled lobby space
Photography: Jon Miller/Hedrich-Blessing

Key:
 1   Lobby
 2   Main worship
 3   Altar
 4   Galleria
 5   Bookstore
 6   Chapel
 7   Chapel
 8   Vestibule
 9   Conference room
10   Office
11   Lounge
12   Exterior storage

0   20ft

7

8

9

AGUDAS ACHIM SYNAGOGUE

Lake/Flato Architects

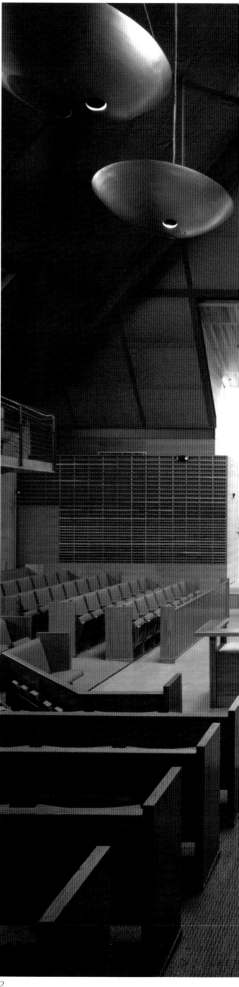

The simple nomadic tents that were the original synagogues contained a sacred space that was filled with light yet grounded solidly to the earth. The program for the synagogue for Agudas Achim in Austin, Texas was to create a space that was both spiritually uplifting and flexible in its function. The material palette for the synagogue, which includes a sanctuary, chapel, and social hall, is primarily Sisterdale limestone, wood detailing, and exposed steel structure.

Four heavy concrete columns support the 40-foot ceiling in the hexagonal sanctuary. Among the requirements for this space was the need to provide intimate seating for 150 people for most services, but also the accommodation of almost 1000 participants during the high holy days. The solution came in the form of a mezzanine that floats delicately above the main space, gently backlit by expansive windows that admit natural light. Branchlike beams sprout from the four columns and support the ceiling whose fabric recalls tent flaps. A skylight forms

the center of the Star of David and sheds a soft glow over the reader's table 40 feet below. Placing the reader's table in the center of the space, as in the Sephardic tradition, also creates a more intimate relationship between the cantor and the congregation.

The east wall holds the ark, which contains the scared torah. The limestone wall recalls the Wailing Wall in Jerusalem, and is lit on three sides by natural light streaming in through strips of glass. This creates the dramatic appearance that the wall and the torah within are bound to the building by rays of light. A wood canopy above reinforces this seemingly tenuous connection.

The architects took inspiration from country buildings and the traditional shapes of eastern European wooden synagogues. The synagogue, social hall, and chapel are housed in simple, low-scaled boxes of stone and metal. The intent is to allow the architecture to support, not overwhelm, the vitality of the place and people within its walls.

1

2

1 Exterior nestles into the landscape
2 Sanctuary roof suggests a tent structure
3 Entry on axis to sanctuary
4 Detail of stair to upper-level seating
Photography: Hester & Hardaway

3

4

GENEVA PRESBYTERIAN CHURCH CHAPEL ADDITION

Dominy + Associates Architects

Geneva Presbyterian Church, a Southern California landmark since its construction in the late 1960s, was designed by Californian architect William Pereira. The congregation embarked on a US$1.1 million expansion to include a new 100-seat chapel and an outside amphitheater designed to take advantage of the courtyard created between the two structures. The space needed to be flexible so that it could adapt to a variety of functions such as weddings, funerals, and youth and preschool activities.

The design challenge was to create a building respectful of the existing contemporary architecture, yet with its own identity. The Laguna Hills site has views of the Saddleback Mountains to the east over the immediately adjacent parking lot. The desired outdoor amphitheater is subject to substantial traffic noise from the adjacent major collector road.

The architects recommended combining the inside chapel and outside amphitheater into one indoor/outdoor assembly space separated with glass doors that slide into pockets at either end, allowing flexibility. Sound walls buffer the outdoor seating area from the road while providing security and enclosure for the courtyard. The new 2240-square-foot chapel is light and airy, with controlled views.

Diagonal fins, incorporated into the design along the east-facing glass, focus the view and lend visual separation to the parking lot while diffusing the morning sunlight. The roof's radiating and splayed straight wood beams and the curved walls reinterpret the softness of the Pereira building. The axial fin wall separating the inside from the outside rises to form a third vertical element completing the campus composition.

Continued

1

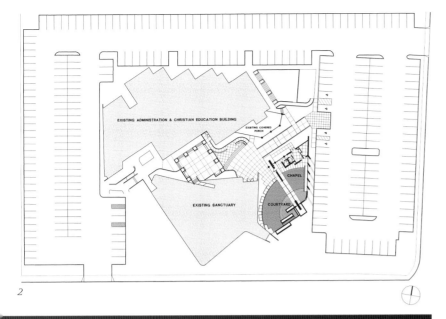

2

1   Existing sanctuary, left, with new chapel, right
2   Site plan
3   Details of new chapel inspired by existing sanctuary
4   Plaza allows outdoor worship

3

4

5   Floor plan
6   Interior of new chapel
Opposite:
    New chapel is light-filled
Photography: Glenn Cormier (1,4,6,7);
Michel Boutefeu (3)

From the inside, the ceiling shape and framing members draw the eye up and outward to the tower of the existing sanctuary. Brick pavers at the courtyard spill over into the seating area inside and are enclosed in acid etched, colored concrete to match the exterior flatwork. The glued/laminated beams and fir wood ceiling are stained a light gray. "Coppera" slate accents walls inside and out. A textured bronze door at the main entry recalls the custom wood doors of the main sanctuary.

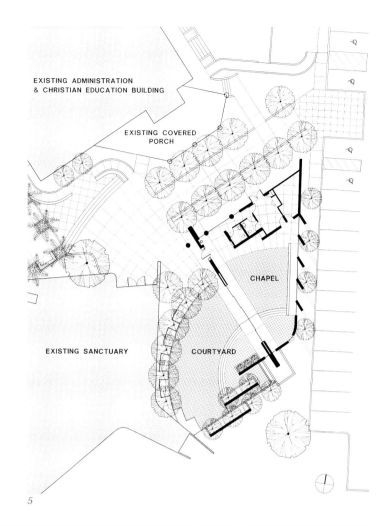

EXISTING ADMINISTRATION
& CHRISTIAN EDUCATION BUILDING

EXISTING COVERED
PORCH

CHAPEL

EXISTING SANCTUARY

COURTYARD

5

6

ST. JOHN VIANNEY CATHOLIC CHURCH

Constantine George Pappas AIA

St. John Vianney Catholic Church is situated on 18 acres in Shelby Township, Michigan. The new facility, upon which Margaret Bouchez Cavanaugh served as liturgical consultant, is constructed around an existing church building, which was ultimately transformed into a multipurpose hall. The design is generated from the concept of a building grid overlaid upon an axis. The brick masonry walls throughout the project highlight the building grid with a special "v" brick stacked vertically every 10 feet on center, terminating at the bottom with a cast concrete accent and at the top with a Mankato stone detail. The endpoints and the intersection of the two axes designate the most important areas in the complex: the entries, the sanctuary, the meditation court, and the baptismal font.

This church is considered to be the largest glue-laminated wood compression-ring structure in the country, and contains approximately 16,000 square feet. Above the central altar is a 2400-square-foot clerestory. Rising to a height of 80 feet at the peak, the clerestory floods the church with natural light. All exposed glue-laminated trusses are designed to articulate and strengthen the axis. The placement of the altar table, central to the space, allows no one person to be farther than 60 feet away from the celebration of Mass. The exterior walls of the church are constructed of masonry, designed to provide lateral stability while affording a feeling of grandeur. The glazing is set deep in the wall, allowing broad shadows to reinforce the punched openings in the thick walls, reminiscent of the heavy masonry walls of the earliest Christian churches.

The overflow/gathering space is positioned between the new church and the multipurpose hall. Full-height glass walls on the north and south exposures of this space allow natural light to filter through the wood structure. The central point is the font. Constructed entirely of ceramic tile, the adult and infant font allows for complete immersion. Three colors of ceramic tile further accentuate the concept of the building grid as it passes through the space.

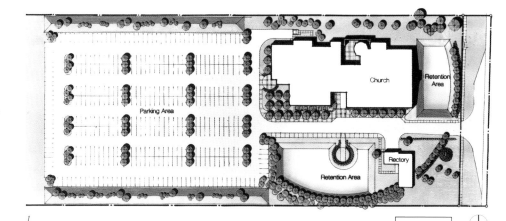

1

0   125ft

2

1 Site plan
2 East elevation of worship space
Opposite:
    Meditation court outside chapel

4   Glassy nature of architecture reveals interior
5   Detail of full-immersion baptismal font
6   Detail of ambulatory around sanctuary

4

5

6

Opposite:
 View from chapel into main sanctuary
8 *Interior of worship space illuminated from above*
9 *Sinuous sounding board over choir*
Photography: Laszlo Regos Photography

8

9

FIRST LUTHERAN CHURCH, ELCA

Dominy + Associates Architects

First Lutheran Church is one of a handful of churches remaining to serve downtown San Diego, California. Throughout its 114-year history, the church has remained in the same vicinity. In the early 1960s a temporary sanctuary was erected on the current site of the church at the corner of Third Avenue and Ash Street. This temporary edifice remained as a sanctuary/fellowship hall for almost 40 years, gradually becoming hidden as high-rise buildings surrounded it. In 1998, the congregation undertook a US$900,000 renovation and addition to the church building. The design challenge was to create an undeniable presence for the church. Also needed was a secure environment for both the congregation and the people it serves.

The complete renovation of the existing 170-seat sanctuary, offices, kitchen, and fellowship hall was augmented by the addition of a new tower, chapel, narthex, a columbarium, a new courtyard, and landscaping.

Inside the front entrance of the 10,475-square-foot building, the narthex and fellowship hall are juxtaposed so that overflow from either space can be accommodated by the other. The interior orientation of the sanctuary is on a diagonal to make the space appear longer and larger. Natural light streams into the sanctuary from three new skylights placed along the diagonal. Natural finishes such as brick, Italian tile, Canadian maple flooring, and exposed wood beams provide warmth.

The new tower rises 67 feet above the chancel. With no height restriction on buildings downtown, the tower is designed so that the scale of the church is in proportion to the adjacent high-rise buildings. Both the tower and chapel have skylights that are illuminated at night, transforming these structures into glowing beacons on the skyline.

The issue of security was addressed by replacing the church's old covered walkways with a new outdoor, open courtyard. Surrounded by concrete bench seating, the courtyard provides ample space for the congregation to socialize. Colored concrete creates a crucifix form that extends invitingly beyond the courtyard onto the city sidewalk.

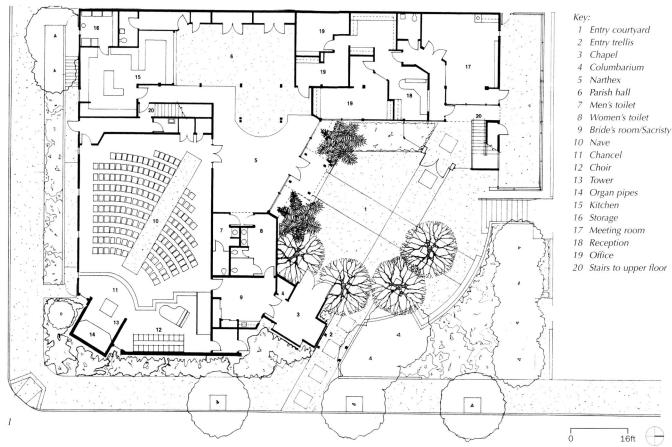

Key:
1. Entry courtyard
2. Entry trellis
3. Chapel
4. Columbarium
5. Narthex
6. Parish hall
7. Men's toilet
8. Women's toilet
9. Bride's room/Sacristy
10. Nave
11. Chancel
12. Choir
13. Tower
14. Organ pipes
15. Kitchen
16. Storage
17. Meeting room
18. Reception
19. Office
20. Stairs to upper floor

0   16ft

1

1 Site plan
2 The church's new wings surround existing buildings
3 Church's inviting presence at night

2

3

4

4 Detail of altar and cross
5 Small chapel near sanctuary
6 Elegant detailing and materials
  used throughout
7 View of main sanctuary
Photography: Glenn Cormier

5

6

7

LIVING WORD CHRISTIAN CENTER

Teng & Associates

The program called for the conversion of a faltering shopping mall in Forest Park, Illinois to a Christian Fellowship Center and Worship Hall for a 5000-member congregation. The Fellowship Center includes classrooms, pre-function gathering spaces, conference facilities, business offices, and a television production studio.

The existing facility was originally built as a torpedo factory during World War II, and was later converted to a shopping mall. The structural bay module and industrial characteristics of the space were not fitting for celebratory worship. However, the spatial/volumetric proportions offered great potential.

The creative response of the design team to the challenge of difficult existing conditions led to the major design theme for the project—the undulating ceiling. Three existing movie theaters, each with different floor slopes, were combined with one level floor to create the central worship hall. Four central columns were removed to provide unobstructed views within the hall, creating a free span of 168 feet. The main floor is flat to allow for multiple seating arrangements and multipurpose activities. Undulating ceiling planes help define the seating areas. The ceiling shape is derived from the original factory skylight configuration. The sinuous forms create interest, establish rhythm, and break down the scale of the hall. At the same time they organize and screen the mechanical systems and sophisticated lighting and sound systems required for broadcast television production. The overall effect is that of a dynamic and uplifting space for celebration.

A bay was added at the south to provide tiered seating. This expansion provided the opportunity to create a new façade and image for the church. This new bay is akin to the narthex in a traditional church, serving as the gathering space before and after the service. The long glass wall admits sunlight and creates a welcoming image for visitors.

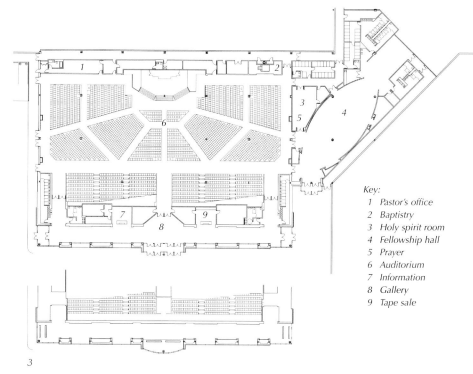

Key:
1 Pastor's office
2 Baptistry
3 Holy spirit room
4 Fellowship hall
5 Prayer
6 Auditorium
7 Information
8 Gallery
9 Tape sale

1 Undulating forms are easily read in section
2 Ceiling helps create an uplifting atmosphere
3 Floor plan
4 Axis on worship area with rolling ceiling overhead
Photography: Russell Phillips

4

DAWOODI BOHRA MOSQUE

Oglesby Greene Architects

This mosque for an Indian-based Muslim community is on a 1.34-acre site in a residential neighborhood in Irving, Texas. The project's diverse 14,000-foot program and modest initial building budget prescribed that both utilitarian material palettes and conventional building systems be cleverly utilized and interwoven into this small, tree-laden site. The program called for four distinct components: a prayer hall, a school for religious studies, a dining/community hall, and the priest's residence.

Budget constraints demanded that "richness" be reinterpreted into the detail, form, and collective composition, versus its traditional materiality. The exception was the selective use of glass mosaics tiled in Fatimid patterns at the prayer hall's entry surround, step risers, and minaret

reveals. Further importance was given to the prayer hall by layering traditional Fatimid elements only in that space, thereby stratifying its significance. Other architectural elements include such items as keel arches with a precise formula for construction; geometric patterned crestings adorning the perimeter walls, parapets, and copings; specific form/composition of minarets and *mihrabs* (prayer niche centered on the *qibla* wall); and unique patterning in mosaics, stone, and wood carvings.

The reinterpretation of the traditional central court is as a public collection space and the physical and spiritual linkage of all four building elements. A fountain is centered in the circular space, symbolic of ablution prior to entering the prayer hall. Its entry lies on axis from the

fountain's center toward Mecca. Each of the four buildings is constructed of conventional wood framing with stucco cladding. Where the building edges touch the circular court, their walls become common load-bearing concrete masonry units, subtly banded and curved to define the space.

The prayer hall accommodates approximately 200 worshippers. The women occupy the peripheral mezzanine area above, while the men align their prayer rugs along the ground floor towards the *qibla*, or direction of prayer toward Mecca, calculated to be N43.5E. The *mihrab* centers on the *qibla* wall's five bays bearing a Koranic scripture carved and gold leafed overhead, and translates, "In the name of Allah, the most gracious, the most merciful."

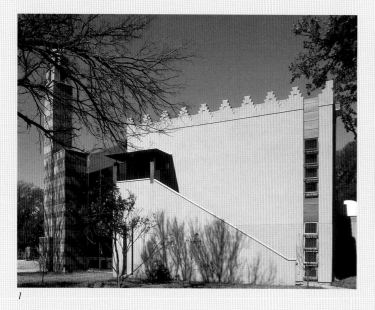

1

2

3

4

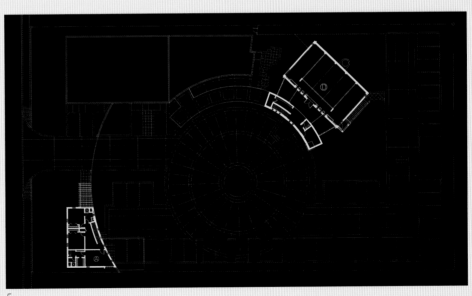

5

6

7

8

Photography: Charles Davis Smith (1-8,10);
Joe M. McCall, FAIA (9,11)

10

9

11

SEASIDE INTERFAITH CHAPEL

Merrill & Pastor Architects

This interfaith chapel for 200 people is built on a prominent site reserved for it in the town of Seaside, Florida on the plan's primary northern axis. The church board asked only that the design serve all members of the community, that it have an element that could be seen from a distance, and that it be made of materials characteristic of the region. The design incorporates light and views of the beautiful natural setting.

The chapel is typically approached from the south on foot, and from the east by car, so it is designed to be seen from either direction. The 68-foot-tall bell tower is a town landmark. The chapel sits on the edge of two communities, serving both. There is a park extending to the south, and a side garden has been created on the east, with a porch that leads to the cemetery. The land to the north is still forested with scrub pines.

The chapel's tall side walls are strengthened on the inside with masonry buttresses to take the wind loading of an unbraced multi-story wall. There are large shear walls in the corners of the structure. The windows of the side elevations reflect the tall space of the sanctuary. The side elevations are partly organized by band courses that correspond to the secondary structural elements girding the interior. The corner shear walls at the loft and altar, slightly offset from the walls of the sanctuary, are sheathed in board-and-batten siding.

The chapel interior is wood and the walls and ceiling are white. The floors are salvaged sinker logs from rivers in northern Florida. The stained flooring material is also used on the altar walls in order to lead the eye there upon entering. The walls and roof are ornamented with a hierarchy of exposed structural members whose sizes reflect the contributing areas of the structural loads. The altar furniture is rendered in heart pine.

1

1   Approach to church by car
2   Section
3   Chapel as it faces the park
Following pages:
    Interior at dusk with indirect lighting
Photography: Steven Brooke

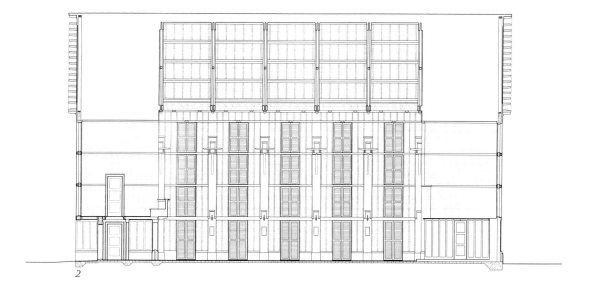

2

3

FIRST PRESBYTERIAN CHURCH
ADDITION AND RENOVATION

Gould Evans Affiliates

The late 19th-century First Presbyterian Church is located across from the capitol building in downtown Topeka, Kansas. The first phase of an expansion plan includes a new multi-function entrance lobby, updated mechanical and electrical systems, and renovated sanctuary, chapel, and children's education spaces. The challenge was to renovate with historical sensitivity and to provide a stand-alone addition to the historic church that would facilitate future additions.

A "jewel box" glass structure now welcomes visitors. At night, the jewel box glows as a beacon for the church's congregation. The existing church has a series of stone buttresses equally spaced along its north elevation.

Incorporating this rhythm, new stone columns continue on the interior and exterior elevations, ultimately framing an existing stained glass window high upon the old north wall. The cut, color, and pattern of the existing stone were carefully matched. The roof structure draws upon materials in the existing sanctuary. Glue-laminated timbers are spaced at the same module as the columns.

The interior renovation began by addressing the north stone wall. Two large penetrations were created, allowing the interior of the existing church to begin to flow into the new lobby space. The new openings were framed in stone and coursed to match the stone openings on the rest of the existing church. A new corridor was

created adjacent to the existing sanctuary and on axis with the eastern wall penetration. Off the corridor a series of new classrooms utilizes bright color schemes and bold patterns symbolizing the focus on youth and vitality.

A series of new arches, proportionally similar to the arch on the existing chancel, utilizes glue-laminated timber from the new interior. These arches march rhythmically between columns around the exterior, following the pattern from the existing building. They are tied to the timber roof beams, again bridging the stone columns and wood roof, earth, and sky. The resulting form references the early Christian symbol of the world in Christ's hands.

1

2

1 New lobby structure from northeast
2 Stone and timber structure is in harmony with existing architecture
3 East elevation
4 Glassy envelope allows ample views inside

3

0   15ft

4

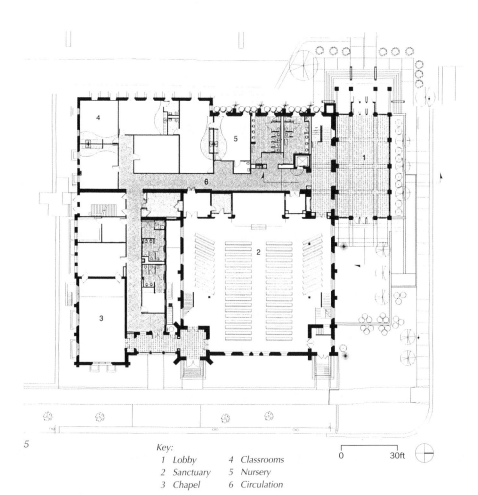

5　First floor plan
6　View of corridor into chapel
7　Entry leading to renovated sanctuary
8　Renovated sanctuary
9　New seating radiates toward altar
Photography: Spillers Photography

5

Key:
1　Lobby　　　4　Classrooms
2　Sanctuary　　5　Nursery
3　Chapel　　　6　Circulation

0　　　　30ft

6

7

8

9

NORTH HILLS CHURCH OF GOD

CCBG Architects

The program for this church in Phoenix, Arizona called for the creation of a 1800-seat sanctuary that responded to the church community's beliefs and needs. It also addressed the difficulties of the terrain, while relating to the existing buildings, which are a combination of stucco, clear glass, and a colonnade of volcanic rock from the adjacent hill. This congregation believes in outreach ministries, and sought a building of unadorned simplicity.

Designed as a black box, the new worship center's material palette includes exposed concrete and masonry, steel, stucco, aluminum, and glass arranged into a series of overlapping wall planes.

The site for North Hills Church of God is dominated by a scoria-strewn hill rising above a parcel that was once used as landfill. The building is anchored into the hill, and in fact the rear seating "sits" on the hill. Fan-shaped seating brings the assembly close together.

The west walls act as a series of barriers to the fierce summer sun. The north and east walls are exposed concrete masonry in stark contrast to the glazed north and east walls of the narthex. Concrete walls mitigate between the building and the hill on the south side. A low, discontinuous concrete masonry wall beginning in front of the building previously used for worship, appears and disappears as it moves from east to west. This wall, stained black to match the rock of the hill, terminates at the base of the cross tower.

A series of concrete seats at the end of a small courtyard between new and existing constructions is used as an outdoor gathering and performing area. This space between buildings recalls a riparian "canyon," shaded during the summer afternoons and sunny during winter mornings.

Key:
1 New worship
2 Existing building
3 Ampitheater
4 Cross
5 Courtyard
6 Gathering
7 Wash
8 Parking
9 Future parking
10 Hill

0   200ft

1

2

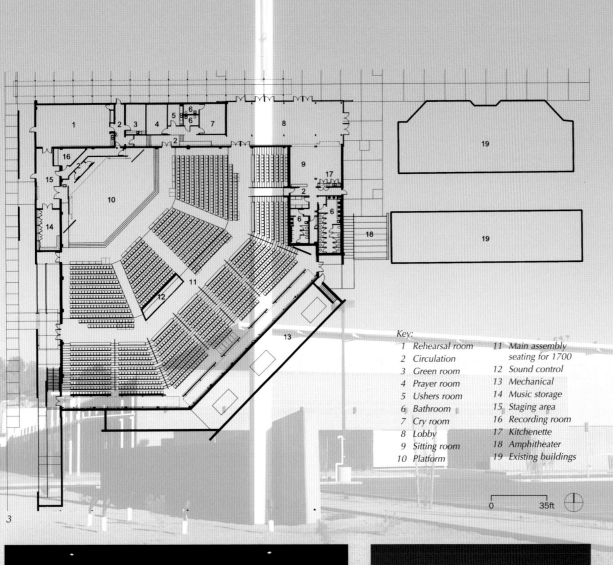

1 Site plan
2 The 1800-seat sanctuary focuses on the stage
3 Floor plan
4 Platform raises celebrants above congregants
5 Cross marks the church from the west
Photography: Chandon Sherwood Thorell

Key:
1 Rehearsal room
2 Circulation
3 Green room
4 Prayer room
5 Ushers room
6 Bathroom
7 Cry room
8 Lobby
9 Sitting room
10 Platform
11 Main assembly seating for 1700
12 Sound control
13 Mechanical
14 Music storage
15 Staging area
16 Recording room
17 Kitchenette
18 Amphitheater
19 Existing buildings

0   35ft

ST. JOHN'S EPISCOPAL CHURCH

Williamson Pounders Architects

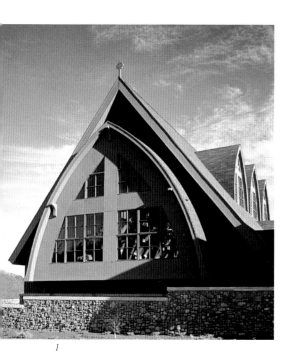

1

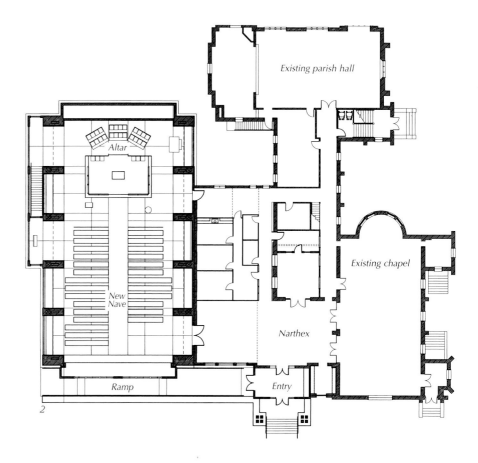

2

For a century, St. John's Church has been a landmark in downtown Johnson City, Tennessee due to its Gothic revival style and distinctive use of river rock stone masonry. To respond to new growth in membership and the revitalization of downtown, the architects were commissioned to design a new main worship space and to provide additional office, sacristy, and classroom space, all on the narrowly constricted urban site.

The new 350-seat nave adjoins the existing narthex and echoes the neo-Gothic character of the existing nave, which is now used as a chapel. A stone ramp heading to a new entry porch provides a processional route as well as access for the disabled. The new addition is clad in cedar shakes and the local river rock was specified to provide visual continuity between the new and old buildings. The gentle pointed arches of the original building are echoed in its new counterpart. A lower-level space was shelled-in to provide for future classroom space.

The new nave is designed as a single dramatic room and features laminated wood arches supported on stone piers; red oak ceilings, casework, and pews; and stained concrete flooring. The interior suggests a gracious place of worship under tree boughs. Acoustical wall panels were custom-stenciled with a pattern developed by the artist and architects. The generous natural lighting provided by the over-scaled dormers and glazed north façade is supplemented by pendant light fixtures designed by the architect. A used pipe organ was purchased and reconfigured for installation in the loft at the south end of the space.

1   *North-facing window and roof dormers admit natural light*
2   *Floor plan*
3   *Regional materials include river rock and cedar shake siding*
4   *New materials include laminated wood arches and stone piers*
5   *Existing church, right, with new church, left*
6   *Natural light floods the nave*
Photography: Tom Raymond

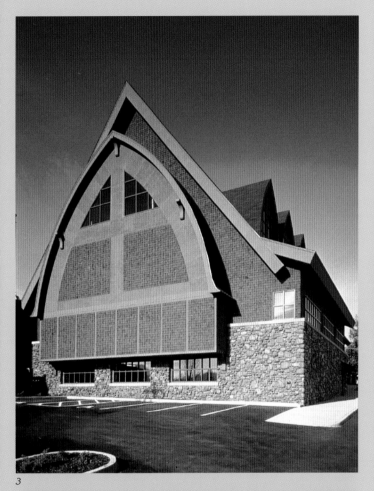

3

4

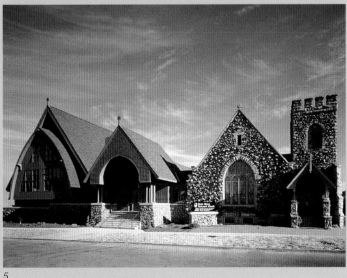

5

6

FIRST GERMAN UNITED METHODIST CHURCH

Fields Devereaux Architects & Engineers

The First German United Methodist Church in Glendale, California is the new home for a congregation that worshipped for more than 100 years at a church in downtown Los Angeles. The original building was appropriated by the City of Los Angeles as part of an urban renewal program.

The church is designed to serve a modestly sized congregation of 150 families—the only Methodist congregation in Southern California that holds services entirely in German. The congregation wanted a contemporary design that looks to the future rather than to the past. At the same time, there was a desire to preserve several important elements of the original church, which included the oak pews, altar, a pipe organ, and two large stained glass windows. These elements were incorporated into the design of the sanctuary, which serves as a jewel box containing precious artifacts.

The site is on a very busy thoroughfare. A walled entry courtyard provides isolation from the noise of traffic and creates a place for outdoor gatherings. The wall is just high enough to screen the views of the commercial properties on Glendale Boulevard from inside the courtyard but allows views to the mountains beyond. The building shapes and is shaped by this courtyard, which is articulated by a trellis that provides shade and defines the edges. The courtyard has become a popular place for weddings and receptions.

The 34,000-square-foot complex includes a sanctuary, social hall, kitchen, offices, Sunday school classrooms, a caretaker's suite, and two levels of underground parking. In order to meet the congregation's limited, fixed construction budget, the architects worked closely with the structural engineer and the general contractor to develop a strategy for constructing the entire building from wood structural elements. This involved using wood mini-lam beams as studs to create the 35-foot-tall, unbraced walls and adding continuous steel strapping as tension-rings to the circular forms near the roofline. This project is an excellent example of a successful collaboration with a general contractor who was brought into the process during the design phase.

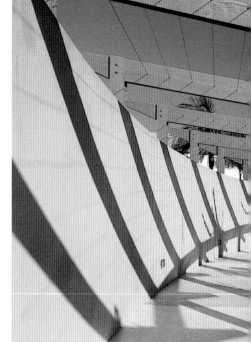

3

4

1

2

1   Church as it faces west
2   View of church across entry plaza
3   Fellowship hall glows at night
4   Trellis surrounds inside of courtyard
5   First floor plan
6   Natural light is admitted from above
7   Sanctuary space has dynamic curves
Photography: Courtesy of architect

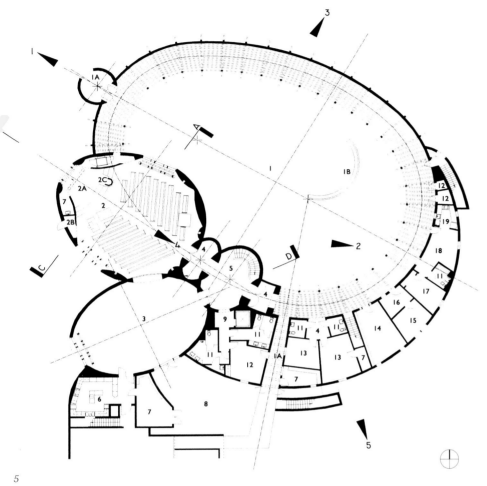

Key:
1	Courtyard	8	Patio
1A	Entry	9	Hall
1B	Bench	10	Bride room
2	Main sanctuary	11	Restroom
2A	Altar	12	Janitor/mechanical
2B	Organ room	13	Classroom
2C	Pulpit	14	Boardroom/library
3	Main fellowship	15	Pastor's office
4	Foyer	16	Office
5	Main vestibule	17	Bedroom
6	Pantry	18	Living/dining
7	Storage	19	Kitchen

5

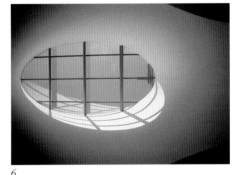

6

7

CHURCHILL BAPTIST CHURCH

Sprinkle Robey Architects

This new 15,000-square-foot multipurpose building for Churchill Baptist Church in San Antonio, Texas uses a restricted palette of stock materials, refined detailing, and simple modulations in massing to fit unobtrusively into its wooded site.

In order to avoid numerous stands of majestic live oak trees, the building is conceived as a large central volume, containing a 6600-square-foot hall, with flanking wings containing classrooms and ancillary functions. An intimate entry court, nestled amidst three twisted oaks, helps to reduce the overall massing and scale of the building.

The classroom wings, with exposed pre-engineered frames forming porches and thus revealing the skeletal framing of the building, create a warm and embracing entry. In addition, the vigor and strength of the oak trees find translation into the machined forms of the structural frames' columns and beams. The stucco wainscot, which wraps only these wings, similarly grounds the building and reduces its scale, relating it to the surrounding residential neighborhood.

The corrugated metal siding, which was selected both for its compatibility with the "metal building" construction technology and for its superb ability to catch and modulate daylight, finds its greatest effect at the south end of the building. Here a simple reorientation of the corrugations mimics the stucco wainscot and breaks the large expanses of wall surface. Cantilevered metal stairs and pipe railings fly from the solid mass of the building to touch down lightly. Clear-span steel frames allow for ease in changing room sizes, with many interior partitions being operable.

Large windows, particularly around the courtyard, create an immediate and intense connection between interior and exterior spaces. This is particularly crucial in the hall given the multipurpose nature of the room. It is envisioned that the hall will serve as a worship space as the congregation outgrows its present sanctuary. In addition, it must meet its functional demands as gymnasium, hall, conference center, and dining area. The large clerestory windows bathe the interior with natural light and transform it from a strictly utilitarian space into one intimately connected to the natural beauty outside.

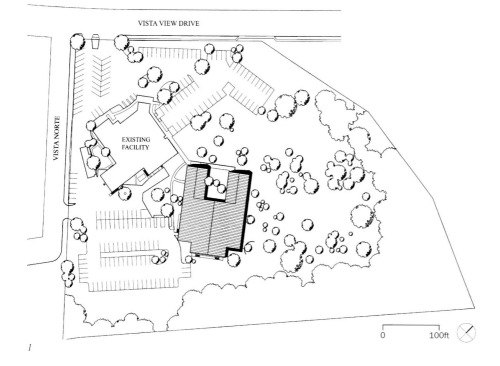

VISTA VIEW DRIVE

VISTA NORTE

EXISTING FACILITY

0   100ft

1

2

1   Site plan
2   Detail of church exterior cladding
3   Floor plan
4   Detail of welcoming courtyard
5   Overview of courtyard
6   Church from the north
Photography: Hester & Hardaway

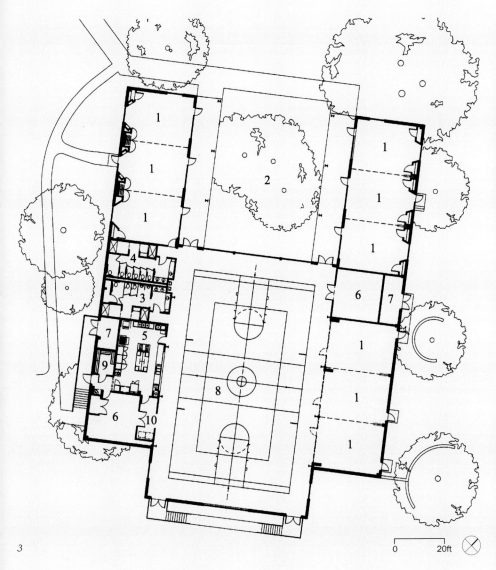

3

0   20ft

Key:
1   Classroom   6   Storage
2   Courtyard   7   Mechanical
3   Men's room   8   Fellowship hall/gym
4   Women's room   9   Pantry
5   Kitchen   10 Vending

4

5

6

GROSSE POINTE UNITED METHODIST CHURCH

Constantine George Pappas AIA

Structure and light underpin the design for this Methodist church in Grosse Point Farms, Michigan. The structure of the church is designed to be a modern expression of a Gothic cathedral, using the warmth of wood and the strength of steel to depict the building's statement in the community. The glue-laminated, wood-frame members ascend toward the building's clerestory only to be taken over by the steel groin vault space frames.

The steel vaults run the full length of the church, reinforcing the worshipper's perspective onto the altar table and the chancel. The steel groin vaults also interpret classic Gothic groin vaults in a truly modern expression. Four limestone cores anchor the building at the four corners and contain support areas on the floor plan. The limestone ashlar pattern, belt-course detailing, and window surrounds match the existing building, which was completed in 1940.

Natural light falls through the space and over the structure from the upper continuous clerestory. At the main floor, full-height glass walls along the side aisles are used to tell the story of Christ's life through stained-glass interpretation. Large picture windows are placed as book ends on both the north and south sides of the church. The northern window opens to the street, allowing the community to share the view of the massive pipe organ and the faith of the United Methodist Church. At night the picture window transforms the church to show its structure.

The final touch within the space is the church's new pipe organ. Designed by both the organ builder and the architect, its purity is expressed in the same way as the building, through natural wood and metal materials. The pipes are positioned above the altar platform to allow projection of sound and to reinforce the view of the entire altar/chancel area.

1

2

1 View into the building at night, through
   clear windows
2 Pipe organ frames wall around chancel
3 Detail of east wall buttresses and roof

3

5

5 Detail of entry with traditional materials
6 Floor plan
Opposite:
   View from nave of neo-Gothic structure
   directly above
Photography: Justin Maconochie/Hedrich-Blessing

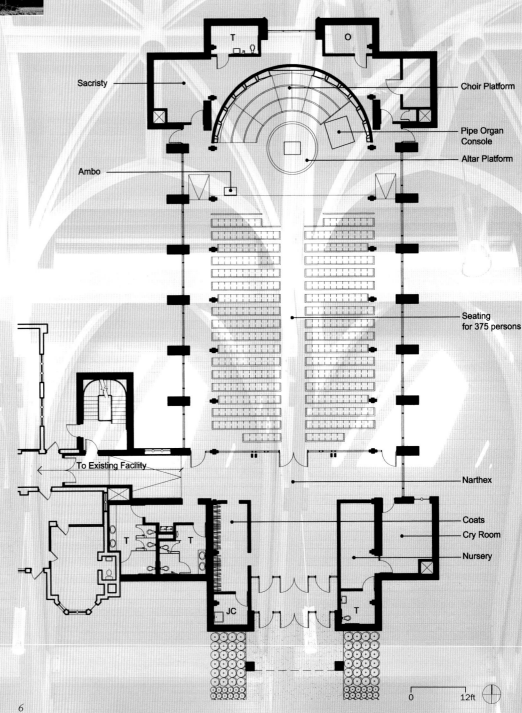

Sacristy

Ambo

To Existing Facility

T O

Choir Platform

Pipe Organ
Console

Altar Platform

Seating
for 375 persons

Narthex

Coats
Cry Room
Nursery

JC T

0   12ft

6

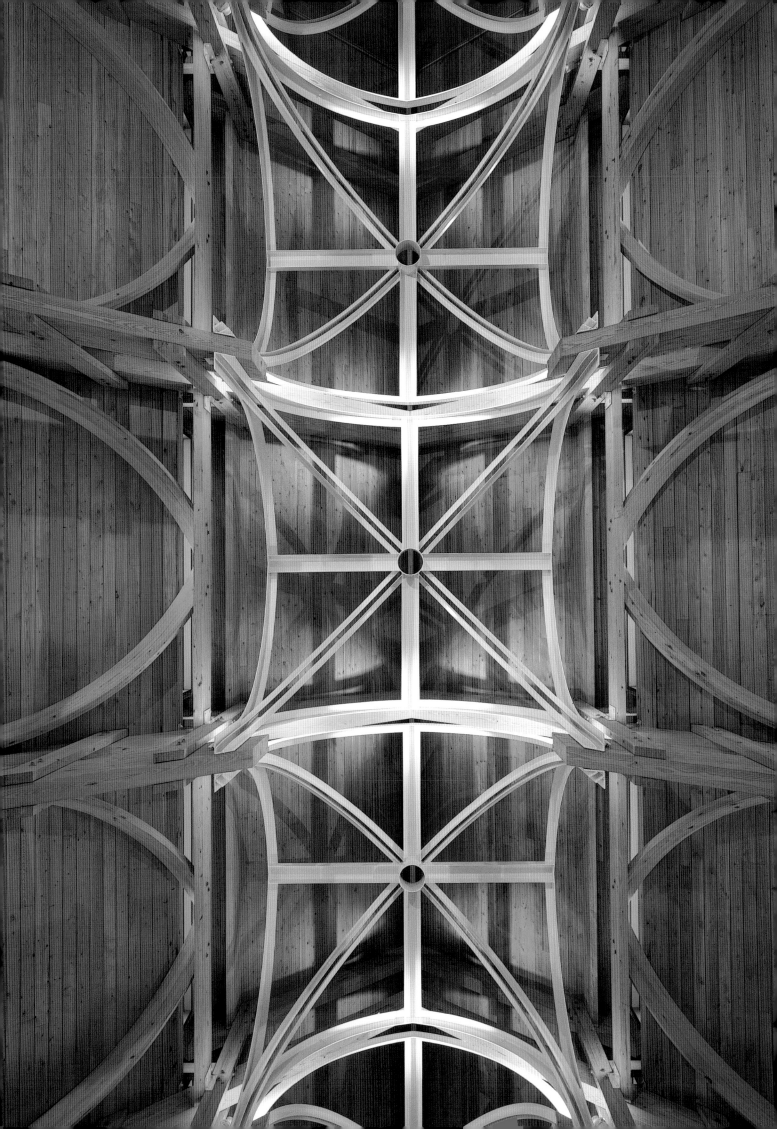

TEMPLE SINAI OF SHARON

Solomon + Bauer Architects

This Reform Jewish congregation outgrew its existing facility and purchased a 49-acre site in Sharon, Massachusetts (all but 5 acres of which were wetlands) to build anew. As a reaction to the existing dark and uninspiring building, the congregation requested that the new building be filled with natural light and have a strong exterior form with which it could identify. Also requested was a significant amount of flexible space for small group meetings or large social events.

Wetlands restrictions and the congregation's desire for an east-facing sanctuary dictated the siting of the building. Necessary storm retention ponds on either side of the building create natural reflecting pools.

Clad in brick and topped with large, curved, copper-clad roof monitors, the sanctuary and social hall dominate the exterior massing, rising above the lower height wood-shingled classroom and administrative areas. Generous window openings in the brick walls contrast with more modestly scaled windows in the wood-shingled skin.

A semicircular skylight accents the lobby entrance to the 200-seat sanctuary. Natural light fills the sanctuary space from both the largely glazed eastern wall and a sizable south-facing window opening. Located under a suspended curved acoustical reflector, the two-level bema accommodates differing ritual and celebratory needs. The lower level projects into the seating area, creating an intimate relationship between the bema and congregation. The upper level contains the freestanding ark wall, seating for bema guests, and alternate locations for the reader's table and lecterns. A curved skylight at the rear of the bema accents the ark wall.

Adjacent to the sanctuary are the foyer and social hall, separated by folding partitions. Served by the linear lobby, these spaces can be used separately or opened as one large space. The social hall can be subdivided into three smaller rooms, each directly accessible from the lobby and each provided with its own curved roof monitor. The lobby, with a large glazed end wall overlooking the site, is designed as an ancillary social space.

1   View of the complex from the south
2   Entry to sanctuary from lobby
3   Floor plan
4   Social hall, with light from above
5   Main sanctuary space with glazed wall
Photography: Bruce T. Martin

1

2

3

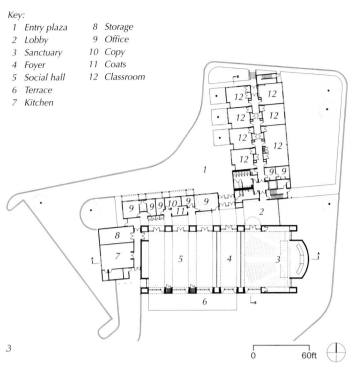

0   60ft

4

5

ATONEMENT LUTHERAN CHURCH, ELCA

Shaughnessy Fickel and Scott Architects

Located in Overland Park, Kansas the worship space and fellowship hall nestle into the sloping site along a major thoroughfare. This arrangement allows both functions to have street frontage, visually inviting each passer-by to view the activity, light, and rituals of the church.

Wrapping around the fan-shaped sanctuary, the narthex provides a wonderful transition between the outside activities and the focused, quiet interior of the sanctuary. On the east elevation, the narthex opens to the outside through large glazed areas. As it embraces the worship space, additional glazing allows views into the lit sanctuary, inviting one to continue the procession of faith.

The worship space unfolds as one enters. The baptismal font visually leads to the cross through its placement and reflection of the water. The variety of space includes the side chapel, which opens to the worship space via a sliding panel door, and the spaces formed by the concrete columns, pews, walls, and balcony. This sense of mystery is also characterized when viewing the art panels from a distance or moving in close to experience their detail.

Animation of the worship space comes from natural light, which articulates the space with changing entry points and intensity throughout the day. At night, interior lights flood the underside of the roof plane allowing the warm glow of the ceiling to be viewed from outside as an invitation to worship. The use of materials is natural and honest to their function.

The chapel accommodates a variety of small services. Its location within the sanctuary, although enclosed, provides a continual connection to the larger assembly. With the sliding wall open, an intimate space is available for the family during a funeral service. The sloping wood wall, with the cross rising from it, has custom-designed joints that allow candles and flowers to be placed in different positions for the full height of the wall. The communion rail is also removable for flexibility in a variety of worship settings.

1   Welcoming façade at dusk
2   View of building's entry, from northeast
3   Entry to narthex
Opposite:
    Balcony offers additional seating

1

2

3

5 Floor plan
6 Seating in sanctuary radiates from altar
7 View from chapel to adjacent sanctuary
8 Altar area in worship space
9 View from font toward altar
10 Light and color are used throughout sanctuary
Photography: Douglas Kahn

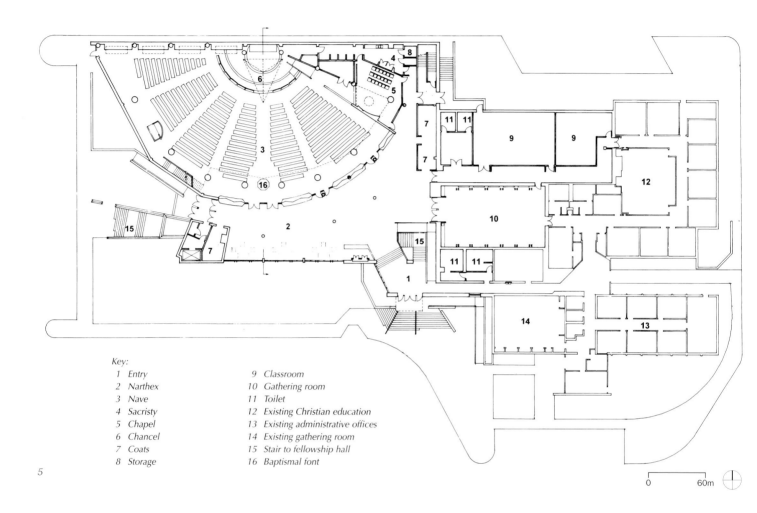

Key:
1	Entry	9	Classroom
2	Narthex	10	Gathering room
3	Nave	11	Toilet
4	Sacristy	12	Existing Christian education
5	Chapel	13	Existing administrative offices
6	Chancel	14	Existing gathering room
7	Coats	15	Stair to fellowship hall
8	Storage	16	Baptismal font

5

0   60m

6

7

8

9

10

HOPE United Methodist Church

Richard Conway Meyer Architect

Situated on the artificial plain of a former sand quarry, this new church in Voorhees, New Jersey was expected to hold its own in a transitional industrial landscape that includes active and abandoned materials plants, microwave towers, light manufacturing, branch banks, and the municipal water tank serving the explosive growth of residential development in every direction. This was to be accomplished within a budget of about US$100 per square foot.

The church views its architecture as a powerful form of evangelical outreach to a transient and secular community. This population may be turned away by traditional ecclesiastical imagery that implies a closed society within. Ecclesiastical images—indeed, all symbolism— are replaced with a sense of the familiar and comfortable: good visibility of available parking spaces, instant identification of the entrance, and an impression of vibrant activity about the site. The transparent front of the worship space is intended to extend these qualities inside; the interior of the building becomes a familiar part of the community landscape.

To reinforce the impression of constant growth, the building presents itself as being perennially incomplete. The large girder in the worship space and the fragile zigzag wall allow easy expansion to the south. The education wing is structured to accommodate a second floor. The entrance canopy can be expanded to twice its size.

Except for the glazed curtain walls, the building is clad entirely in an exterior insulation finish system on a steel frame. The final cost of construction, exclusive of site work, was US$106 per square foot.

Key:
1   Vestibule
2   Lobby
3   Reception
4   Work room
5   Office
6   Conference
7   Worship
8   Storage
9   Coats
10 Classroom
11 Nursery
12 Cry room
13 Kitchen

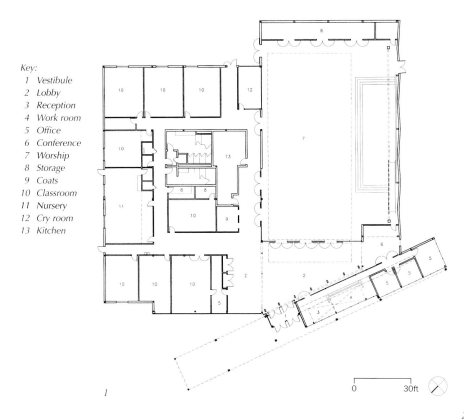

0   30ft

1

2

3

4

1 Floor plan
2 Raised dais for performance and worship service
3 From the parking lot, the building opens to visitors
4 View of the glassy building at night
5 The worship space is revealed through glazed wall
Photography: Tom Crane Photography

5

New Hope Missionary Baptist Church

Harding Associates

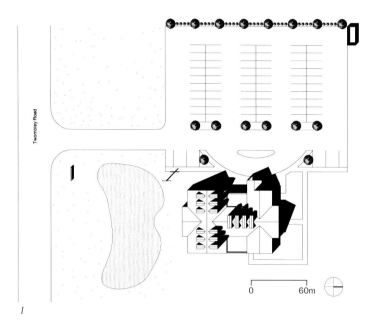

1

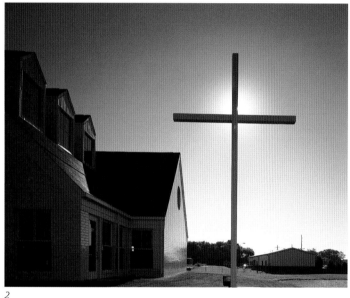

2

Design intentions for New Hope Missionary Baptist Church are rooted in African-American culture and history. The design of this church in DeKalb, Illinois is derived from vernacular "Spirit Houses" in South Carolina and Georgia, where slaves gathered for liturgical celebration and expression. These humble churches were simple whitewashed, wood-framed structures with unadorned interiors. Daylighting, symbolic of God's enlightenment, permeated the worship space and created an ever-changing tapestry for worship and cultural celebration. New Hope Missionary Baptist Church seeks to recognize African-American heritage by building upon the typology of the "Spirit House."

The church serves a predominantly African-American congregation. Major program components of the 9400-square-foot church include a 300-seat sanctuary, a gathering

space/multipurpose hall, a library, classrooms, and offices. Simple and straightforward vernacular construction technology is utilized for cost considerations and to reflect the origins of African-American religious architecture in this country. Simple vernacular forms fit well with the regional rural architecture.

Substituting for the whitewashed clapboard siding of the "Spirit Houses" is white-glazed brick for a durable exterior envelope, appropriate to the climate of northern Illinois. White-glazed brick gives the church a glowing presence on the green rural landscape. Sunrises and sunsets are reflected in the glossy, glazed surface, giving the building an ephemeral quality that varies with the time of day and seasons.

The building is sited to overlook a pond that provides for stormwater retention and creates a natural reflecting pool for the building.

The colors and materials of the main worship space reflect those utilized in African cultural icons. An accent wall forms the backdrop for the 40-person choir and wood pulpit, and intersecting gable shapes create a simple, yet dynamic volume for worship. The fan-shaped seating in the sanctuary wraps around the platform to foster a sense of community within the congregation. The building is organized around the central gathering space, which doubles as a multipurpose hall. A stained-glass image of "Black Jesus" separates the library from the gathering space.

1   Site plan
2   Cross near building entrance
3   Section
4   View from southeast, with dormer roofs

3

4

5

5   Glazed wall from sanctuary to gathering space
6   Sanctuary allows seating close to pulpit

6

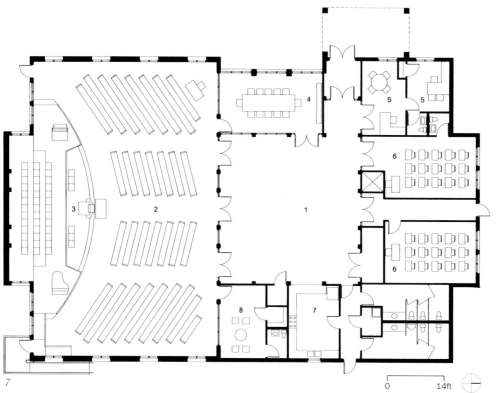

7 Floor plan
8 Sanctuary receives natural light from above
9 Gathering space just off main entry
Photography: Craig Dugan/Hedrich-Blessing

Key:
1 Gathering/multi-purpose space
2 Main worship
3 Platform
4 Library/meeting room
5 Office
6 Classroom
7 Kitchen
8 Choir

0   14ft

7

8

9

OLD ST. JOSEPH'S CATHOLIC CHURCH

Hammel, Green and Abrahamson

Old St. Joseph's Catholic Church, which serves as the chapel for St. Norbert College in DePere, Wisconsin, was completed in 1888 and endured a 1970s renovation during which all sculpture, ornament, and artwork were removed. The program called for the renovation of the chapel to reflect the changing Roman Catholic liturgy, and the construction of an addition to accommodate much needed support spaces.

Designed by James Shields of HGA, with Fr. Richard Vosko as liturgical consultant, the chapel's new entry opens into a skylit atrium gathering space, grafted onto the east façade of the old chapel. A new support building on the opposite side of the atrium contains restrooms, meeting spaces, new mechanical space, kitchens, and storage spaces.

The new atrium gathering space incorporates the historic brick façade of the chapel as an interior façade. A new limestone font was placed in this atrium, composed of a solid block of regional stone. Stone steps allow for the lower pool to be used for adult immersion, while infant baptisms can occur in the small upper pool. The presence of the font also helps to form a threshold condition for entry into the main chapel space.

Inside the main worship space, the former linear plan with the altar distant from the congregation has been transformed into a flexible and centralized plan. The old vestry, sacristy, and apse were demolished to increase the chapel's capacity. The main worship space is completely renovated, including the removal of both the plaster ceiling and walls, revealing the original brickwork and timber trusses. Eight refined stained-glass windows—considered a treasure by the parish—are incorporated into the space, mounted on floating frames. This allows ample daylight to enter the space from around the stained glass, brightening the once dark interior.

From the atrium gathering space, a direct axis connects to a new octagonal Oratory Chapel, which also includes space for Eucharistic Reservation. Iron gates by Wisconsin craftsman Rick Findora separate the space from the niche for the tabernacle.

Key:
1 Worship
2 Atrium gathering
3 Oratory chapel
4 Tabernacle
5 Parlor
6 Kitchen
7 Sacristy
8 Toilet

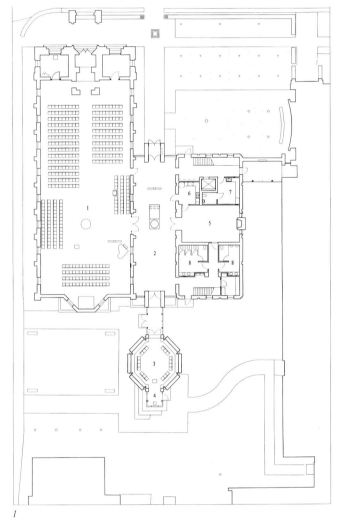

1

2

3

1   Floor plan
2   Exterior of Oratory Chapel
3   Rear of chapel, with Oratory Chapel at right
4   View of glass-roofed gathering space
5   Interior of renovated chapel
6   Stained-glass windows in chapel
7   Tabernacle in Oratory Chapel
Photography: Steve Mofle

4

5

6

7

TEMPLE RODEF SHALOM

James William Ritter Architect

After 30 years in the same facility, this very active Jewish congregation in Falls Church, Virginia found it necessary to expand its synagogue to include a large social hall, meeting rooms, and additional classroom space for both religious and secular education.

While attending back-to-back Yom Kippur services at the temple, the architect observed that the members invariably made contact with their friends as they came or went, to the extent that the small lobby and entrance walk were completely clogged with traffic. It was obvious that the temple members needed space that allowed for social contact and even encouraged it. This "pre-function space" was not a part of the building program as developed by the building committee, but it was clearly an opportunity to enhance the experience of arriving or leaving the temple and to transform the architectural character of the building appropriate to its stature as the center of the Jewish community in Northern Virginia.

The grand hall and entrance terraces are sized and arranged to accommodate 500 people, as well as small groups of two or three. The entrance steps are interrupted by a large landing and a bench that is intended to foster serendipitous encounters.

Pre-function spaces at Temple Rodef Shalom are punctuated with statuesque columns. The columns modulate these spaces and make them honorific by their presence throughout. To relate the building to Jewish history, there is a series of wall fragments made of stone imported from Israel—the same stone as found in the ancient walls and buildings of Jerusalem. The congregants experience this Jerusalem Wall each time they visit the synagogue, akin to ways in which people experience the ancient ruins among the hills of old Jerusalem.

1

1 Social hall wing, with classrooms below
2 At night, building becomes a luminous forest
3 Welcoming canopy held aloft by muscular columns

2

3

4

5

6

4   Curved stone wall distinguishes library space
5   View down grand hallway past library
6   View from interior to outdoor terrace area
7   Sanctuary's structure is expressive
Photography: Hoachlander Davis Photography

7

LUTHERAN CHURCH OF HOPE

RDG Bussard Dikis

1

2

This church in West Des Moines, Iowa was organized as a new Lutheran mission congregation in 1993 with a membership of around 50 people. By the turn of the century, church membership was more than 3000, with an average attendance of 2400. One reason for this growth is the congregation's commitment to living and teaching the Bible. The Great Commission is woven into the church's mission statement and enlivens the spirit of the place on a daily basis. The design of the church and property is intended to express and strengthen this spirit of reaching out and being Christ-centered.

This 37,000-square-foot building is meant to be an evangelist. It is meant to be of today and express the Holy Spirit, not traditional church imagery. The building maintains the vision statement of the church by being Christ-centered. The building and parking are organized around a central drum. This drum is topped by a skylight and cross that serve as beacons to the surrounding suburban residential community. All entrances follow the cross in plan and lead people to the central gathering place—the community space of the church. The building is meant to be energetic, alive, and transparent. The building glows and welcomes the congregation at night. Its forms reach out during the day.

The worship space is designed mainly for contemporary worship with audiovisual systems and live band music. This space will become the café of the future larger church when the subsequent worship space is built. The building, therefore, is also built as a core from which other additions will grow. Because of this church's growth, the building is designed to be as flexible as possible. The rear walls of the worship space fold or slide away to become one large space. The curved doors can slide 360 degrees to create clear viewing areas and create multiple informal learning/community settings.

The building is constructed with modest materials: metal wall panels to recall the scales of fish, recycled cement board siding, brick, and integrally colored concrete floors.

1   Sloped wall distinguishes building form
2   View of main entry from south
3   Section-looking towards worship space
4   Gathering area is marked with central skylight
5   Worship space with planar ceiling
6   Building as it faces northwest
7   Floor plan
Photography: Assassi Production

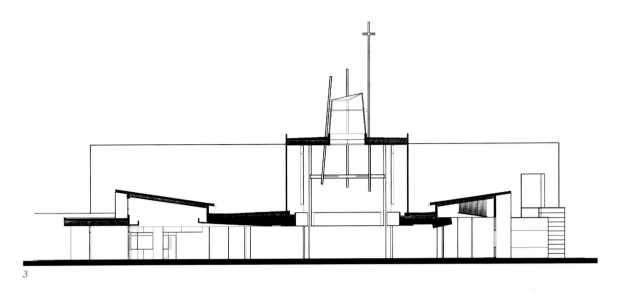

3

4

5

6

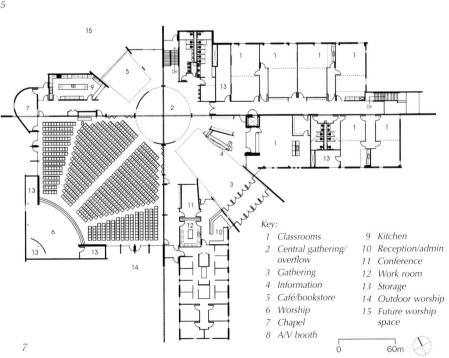

7

Key:
1 Classrooms
2 Central gathering/
   overflow
3 Gathering
4 Information
5 Café/bookstore
6 Worship
7 Chapel
8 A/V booth
9 Kitchen
10 Reception/admin
11 Conference
12 Work room
13 Storage
14 Outdoor worship
15 Future worship
   space

0   60m

SIXTH CHURCH OF CHRIST, SCIENTIST

Metropolitan Design & Building Company

The Sixth Church of Christ, Scientist is a renovation of a humble 5000-square-foot, single-story brick storefront building that provides meeting space as well as a reading room for the congregation. The aim in transforming this nondescript building was to satisfy the congregation's desire to present a stronger identity in the community. The urban neighborhood in North St. Louis, Missouri where Sixth Church is located has managed to stabilize itself after suburban flight took its toll, but it had deteriorated from what was once a vibrant community built on solid middle-class values. The congregation looked beyond their immediate surroundings and envisioned something that would inspire the community.

The new wall elements of the building's façade presented at varying angles create a welcoming and protecting appearance with their clean, crisp white planes, like angelic hands or wings enfolding the congregation and uplifting the community. The building not only provides for the church's physical needs but also addresses the human need for inspiration and expresses the vitality of the congregation in their neighborhood.

From the front and formal entry, which is the most visually compressed area of the project, several opportunities unfold. The entry into the auditorium is flanked on the right by a shrouded coatroom and on the left by the reading room— a quiet, almost library-like space for both the study and sale of Christian Science literature.

The primary design gesture for the interior is focused through the auditorium entry and toward the reader's platform where church services are conducted. This focus is further endorsed by an overhead sculptural element, an oculus, which conceals lighting that flows forward in the direction of the reader's podium and by the expansive expression of the auditorium volume itself. The oculus form is eccentrically balanced by an indirect lighting cove that makes use of an unavoidably exposed structural steel beam and provides general illumination throughout the auditorium. This lighting treatment employing exposed overhead steel beams is reiterated at various locations throughout the project.

1

1   View of church from Gimblin
2   Church as it faces Broadway
3   Ceiling of auditorium
4   View toward entry at corner
5   Detail of display window on Broadway façade
6   Reception desk offers display of books
Photography: Sam Fentress

2

3

4

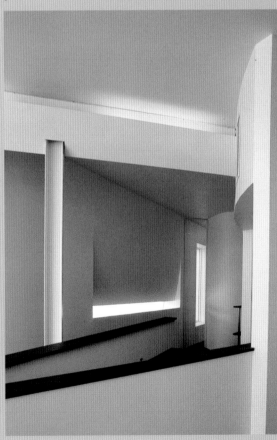

5

6

ST. THERESA CHURCH

Keefe Associates

The site of this new 300-seat church is a narrow lot sloping down from the main street of the country town of Sherborn, Massachusetts, southwest of Boston. Surrounding buildings, both public and private, date from the late-18th to mid-20th centuries, and are constructed mainly in the tradition of wood-frame New England village churches. The design goal was to respect this historic context while meeting the extensive contemporary needs and modest financial resources of a growing Roman Catholic parish.

The 16,000-square-foot building program combines a worship space, a social hall, religious education classrooms, parish offices, and a residence for the pastor. The plan and massing of the building are arranged to maintain appropriate separation of public, semi-public, and private spaces within a unified whole. The main worship space, social gathering areas, and bell tower dominate the public face of the

building, while parish administrative offices and the pastor's quarters occupy an attached, domestically scaled volume at the back of the site, sheltered by dense woodland.

Worshippers enter through a stonewalled garden, pass into an interior gathering space centered on the baptismal font, and then into the nave of the church itself. Seats surround the altar and the skylit cross. The exposed laminated timber frame roof gives warmth to the worship space and evokes the inside of an upturned wooden boat or ark—common imagery in Christian churches. Architectural trim is minimal in the interior, in keeping with the spare, farmhouse vernacular.

Liturgical furnishings of cherry, oak, and bronze have tree-like, bracketed legs so as to appear firmly rooted in the earth as they reach out to support their assigned functions. The interior is intended to be simple, bright, comfortable, and intimate.

1

2

1   Entry from parking lot leads to social spaces
2   View of church from southwest, facing approach
3   Elevation

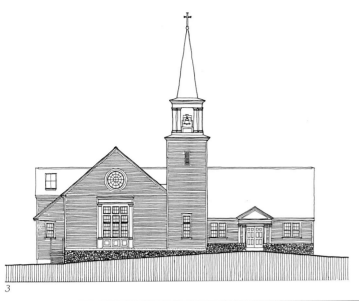

3

4 Chapel for the Reservation of the Eucharist
   is just west of the main altar
5 Upper floor plan
6 Interior of sanctuary has barn-like structure
Photography: Douglas Gilbert

4

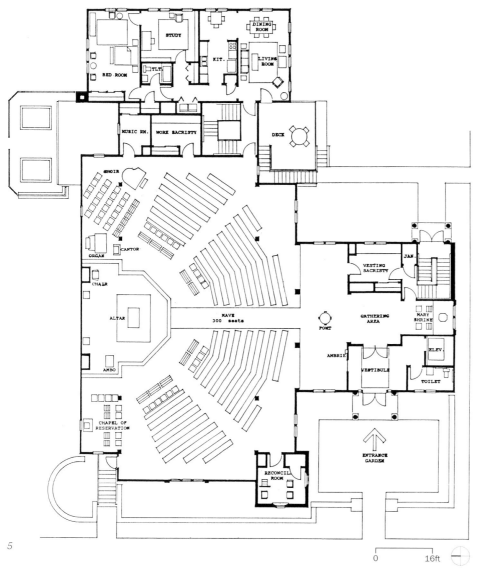

5

6

0   16ft

OAK HILLS CHURCH OF CHRIST

Rehler, Vaughan & Koone

Oak Hills Church of Christ in San Antonio, Texas blends technology and tradition to provide a contemporary worship experience. The 102,000-square-foot building contains a 2800-seat multipurpose sanctuary and three educational wings off a spine that resembles a shopping mall parti. The educational component of the building consists of a nursery/primary wing, an adult/administrative wing, and a primary/youth wing.

In the large, open interiors along the spine, one finds check-in/gathering locations into each wing. Much attention is given to the acoustical properties of each area, particularly the main worship space. This space incorporates various sound technologies that allow it to perform for both spoken word and full accompaniment singing. The main worship space has proven so successful that the church has produced several high-quality recordings from live performances.

As an integral part of its youth and local mission programs, Oak Hills Church of Christ includes a competition-grade gymnasium. The gym has portable basketball goals and provisions for volleyball standards. Until construction of the sanctuary building, worship services were held in the gym and utilized retractable bleachers with theater-type seats.

Unlike many large church complexes, the exterior of Oak Hills responds to the regional architectural language. Limestone, stucco, brick, and metal roofing recall the materials common to this part of the Texas hill country, and give this church its vernacular flavor. Shaded overhangs provide protected areas where one can find respite from the hot sun, and they capture cool breezes that flow around the building.

1

1 East elevation overlooks the countryside
2 Canopied entry to multipurpose worship wing
3 Worship space can be used for sports events
4 View of education wing and two-story circulation space
5 View toward dais in worship area
Photography: Leigh Christian

2

3

4

5

ST. JOHN'S EPISCOPAL CHURCH

Carney Architects

This project is located on a two-acre site near the town square in Jackson, Wyoming. The 11,512-square-foot building includes a new sanctuary, parish hall, and education wing for an expanding congregation that had outgrown its beloved historic log chapel. Two primary goals of the client were the preservation of a park-like open space and the harmonious integration of the new structure into the context of the existing historic log buildings. The original chapel, listed in the National Historic Buildings Register, and the adjacent parish house remained untouched. The preserved historic buildings provide an important link to the past and set the architectural tone for the new construction.

The siting of the new building next to the existing structures creates a cloistered courtyard facing west that serves as the main entry to all church functions. The apse of the church faces east in accordance with liturgical tradition, and presents the public façade to the park and main street of the town.

The architectural concept for the new building is driven primarily by the need to fit into the historic context of log buildings, simple roof forms, and low eaves, as a symbol of downtown Jackson. The 250-seat main sanctuary is constructed of chinked lodgepole logs in traditional basilica form with a structure of log scissor trusses. The log apse, the central architectural element on the east side of the building, has an upper story of cedar shingles and a high window illuminating the altar.

Clerestory dormers on the north and south bring light to the red birch-paneled sanctuary and provide celestial views. A half-round window brings high western light into the sanctuary through the narthex. A small chapel off the sanctuary serves as a columbarium and baptistery and provides a tangible symbol of the circle of life and death.

1 Church's west-facing entrance is warm
2 Sanctuary with its expressive structure and filtered sunlight

1

2

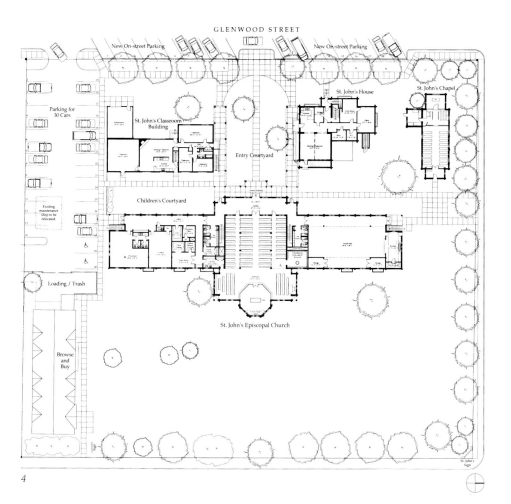

GLENWOOD STREET

New On-street Parking · New On-street Parking

Parking for 30 Cars

St. John's Classroom Building

St. John's House

St. John's Chapel

Entry Courtyard

Children's Courtyard

Existing maintenance shop to be relocated.

Loading / Trash

Browse and Buy

St. John's Episcopal Church

4

5

6

Opposite:
  Chancel is defined by raised floor and
  structure above
4 *Floor plan*
5 *Font shares space with columbarium*
6 *View of church from northeast, as it nestles*
  into context
Photography: Roger Wade

CATHEDRAL OF ST. JOHN THE EVANGELIST

Hammel, Green and Abrahamson

As the principal or "mother" church of the Roman Catholic diocese and the site of the official chair of the archbishop, the Cathedral of St. John the Evangelist in Milwaukee, Wisconsin is a place of ceremony and celebration, repose and reflection. In the more than 150 years since the cathedral opened its doors it has undergone several changes and alterations. Its recent restoration returns the cathedral to its rightful place as a "Jewel of the City," a center of worship, culture, art, and beauty.

Architect James Shields and others on the HGA design team embraced the cathedral as an extraordinary and beautiful house of worship.

Working with liturgical consultant Fr. Richard Vosko, they restored the environment to its past glory while making the church more accessible to the community at large by integrating the complex into the life of the city.

The sanctuary has been transformed with a respect for history and religious expression using colors, lights, and materials. In addition to increased seating capacity within the sanctuary, careful attention was paid to the interior workings of the building. The cathedral's mechanical, electrical, and HVAC systems, as well as the lighting and sound systems, were all upgraded.

A restored building off the cathedral garden to the east will house additional meeting space and administrative offices for the cathedral parish. This will provide space to better accommodate the parish's outreach and service ministries, such as the Door Ministry for homeless men. The historic convent building will also be renovated as a resource center for homeless women and their children. The cathedral grounds are barrier-free with multi-use green space open to the public.

1 *Altar table becomes center of worship space*
2 *Side aisles use sensitive lighting*
3 *Detail of classical ornament*
4 *Sculpture encircles altar table*
5 *Elegance of Reconciliation Room*
6 *View from font to altar*
Photography: John J. Korom Photography

1

2

3

4

5

6

ROTH CENTER FOR JEWISH LIFE

R.M. Kliment & Frances Halsband Architects

The Roth Center provides facilities for the cultural, academic, and social activities of Jewish students and faculty at Dartmouth College and for the Upper Valley Jewish Community. It is the only Jewish congregation in the small town of Hanover, New Hampshire. The site is on a residential street at the edge of the campus. The exterior of white-painted wood clapboard siding, with a green-shingled roof, fits into the residential New England village context.

The 10,500-square-foot center includes a large sanctuary divisible into a smaller sanctuary and dining space, a library, classrooms, nursery, kosher kitchen, student lounge, game room, and offices. The sanctuary faces the street, welcoming the community. The library faces the campus, welcoming students. The lawn to the north is an outdoor gathering place and play area for the nursery. The meadow to the east is a recreation space shared with the adjacent dormitories and sorority house.

The building is organized around the sanctuary and the library, the sacred spaces of the building. These two volumes are connected by a double-height gallery with clerestory windows. The complex geometry of the ceiling forms a complete and focused compositional element for both spaces, and incorporates lighting and partition tracks. The gallery connects the two entrances, joins the spaces of the building, and is a gathering space for the campus and community. The sanctuary is used for worship services, Sabbath dinners, community events, and celebrations. The ark contains torahs and liturgical furniture, which can be moved about the room in a variety of configurations, encouraging informal interactive worship. A movable partition divides the room, creating a smaller worship space lit with enormous clerestory windows, and a dining space with windows opening to the adjacent lawn.

The building includes passive solar heating of the gallery space, natural ventilation and operable windows for cooling, ceiling fans to prevent stratification of air, extensive use of natural light, and use of renewable materials such as the cork floors in the sanctuary.

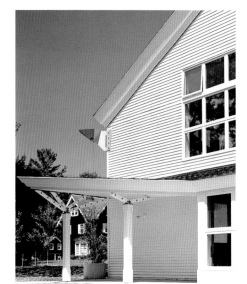

1

2

1   Entry porch into sanctuary wing
2   Interior of sanctuary at dusk
3   Center as it faces the campus to the southwest
4   Light-filled gallery connecting two entrances
5   Main level floor plan
6   Sanctuary with natural light and roof structure
Photography: Peter Aaron/Esto (1,3,6); Cervin Robinson (2,4)

3

4

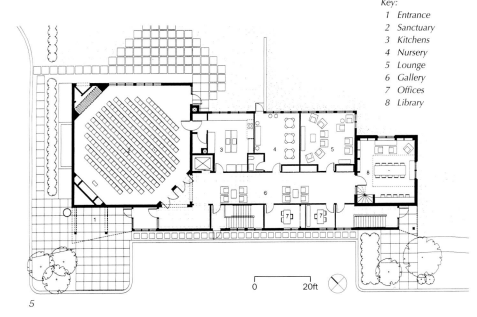

0   20ft

5

6

CHURCH OF THE NATIVITY

Shaughnessy Fickel and Scott Architects

The congregation for this Roman Catholic church in Leawood, Kansas wanted a traditional-looking church with a seating arrangement that would allow everyone to be in close proximity to the altar and ambo. The design approach was to use structural form rather than applying stylistic designs to a contemporary church. The proximity of congregation to celebrant eliminated the need for a traditional nave and resulted in the adaptation of the apse as an ancient form modified to meet contemporary needs.

The exterior stucco walls set on a limestone base are accented by tall, narrow windows piercing the roofline and drawing one's eye up to the central lantern. These windows extend inward and are the reverse of a typical bay window in plan. The configuration diffuses and reflects the light onto the adjacent interior walls, giving a soft glow to the perimeter. The center of the assembly is flooded with diffused natural light from the lantern. A large skylight over the sanctuary allows direct sunlight (controlled and filtered by a suspended baffle system) to penetrate the sanctuary while creating a contemporary baldachin. The tabernacle niche is cantilevered beyond the exterior of the sanctuary allowing natural light to enter from the sides. Large, contemporary glulam arches span the nave and provide support for eight smaller glulam arches of the drum, which in turn support the glulam arches of the lantern.

The architect-designed liturgical appointments complete the architectural unity of the worship space. The altar expresses its dual function as holy table and altar of sacrifice while the ambo symbolizes the Word of the Lord flowing out to the assembly. Similarly, the baptismal font utilizes a symbolic hexagon representing the eighth day as that of the resurrection. The design of the tabernacle draws on Old Testament images of the temple being the dwelling place of the Lord and the cast bronze tabernacle lamp reinforces this tie.

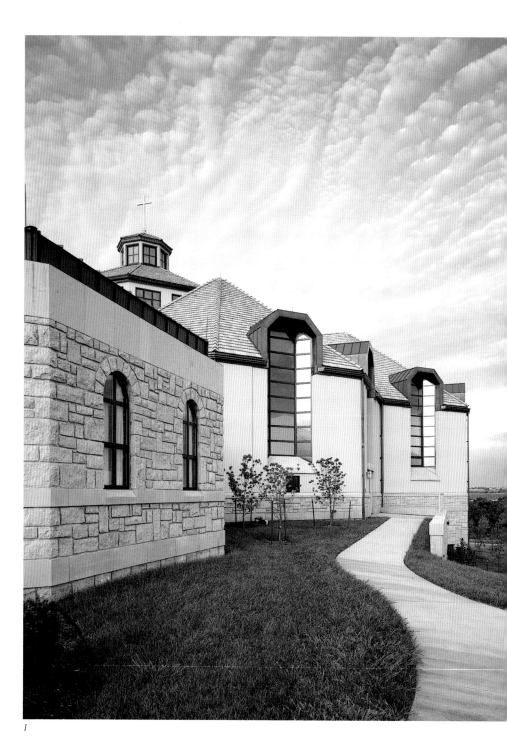

1

1   Detail of exterior materials, including natural limestone
2   Church as it faces main vehicular entrance
3   View of church from northwest

2

3

4

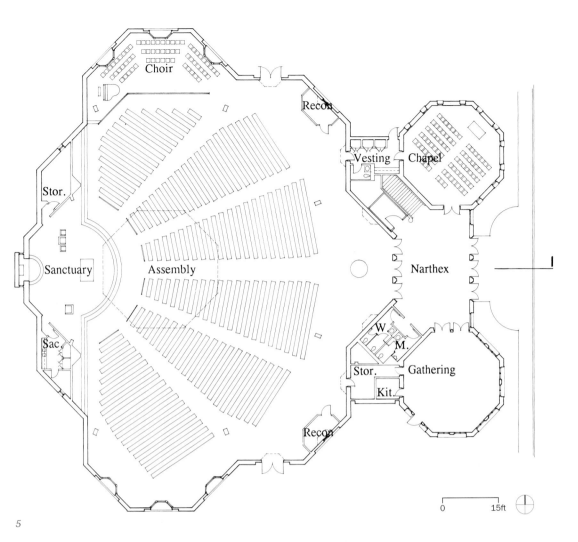

5

6

7

4 Sanctuary is flooded with natural light
5 Main level floor plan
6 Reverse bay windows in sanctuary
7 View into lantern over the sanctuary
Photography: Architectural Foto Graphics

ST. DAVID'S EPISCOPAL CHURCH

Uekman Architects

This church is located on seven acres in Loudoun County, Virginia, a location which is experiencing intense suburban development. The site includes the ruins of an historic Civil War-era chapel that, in addition to Sunday worship, was once used as a school for girls and was a stop along the Underground Railroad. The ruins stand in a grove of tall oak trees.

The program for the new worship center called for nave seating of 425, an entry narthex for gathering, two classrooms, associated storage rooms, and 140 parking spaces. The nave was to accommodate concerts, lectures, and small plays as well as worship. The design would also allow for expansion of the administration and education wings, with the central cupola eventually serving as the cross axis between the separate programs.

The new building is both flexible in use and structured in its Anglican traditions, with a strong sense of familial gathering. The design preserves an historic oak grove to celebrate the beauty of the land as part of the worship experience. The stuccoed wall of the nave assists in defining the oak grove as an outdoor room, sheltering it from views of parking. The 1300-square-foot narthex opens to the nave via glass sliding doors, allowing it to accommodate an additional 100 chairs. Large windows open the nave to the oaks and to views of the chapel ruins, now scheduled for restoration. The canopy of tall trees filters the sunlight from the south-facing façade.

A full-immersion font dominates the center of the nave. Developed in collaboration with Reverend McWhorter, the font is designed to support the casket during funeral services. The open altar area lacks formal communion stations, reinforcing the sense of community around the altar table. Finishes are simple, and structural and mechanical elements are exposed whenever possible. Colored concrete floors, a poured concrete baptistery, faux stucco siding, and prefabricated industrial trusses were chosen for low maintenance, speed of installation, and low cost.

1

1   On axis with entrance at night
2   View of church from northwest
3   Detail of bell tower near church entrance
4   Altar table and cross carry theme of simple
    interior
5   Floor plan
6   Axial entry to sanctuary
7   Detail of baptismal font
Photography: Prakash Patel

2

3

Key:
1 Narthex
2 Nave
3 Baptistry
4 Children's chapel
5 Audiovisual room
6 Sacristry
7 Infants room
8 Toddlers room
9 Storage
10 Mech. court
11 Terrace
12 Muro di Camponelli

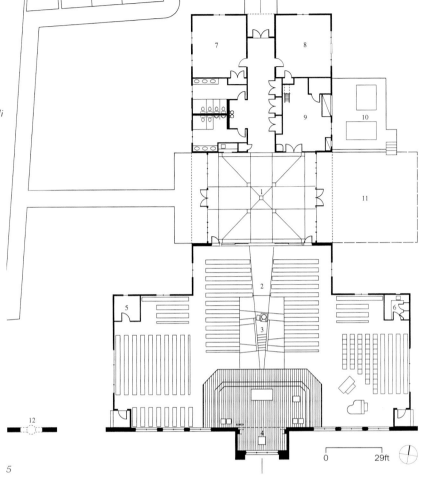

4

5

6

7

ST. IRENE CHURCH

Harding Associates

The main components of the building program for St. Irene Church in Warrenville, Illinois include a eucharistic hall, daily liturgy chapel, reconciliation chapel, gathering space, sacristy, and music room. Materials indigenous to the Midwest region, such as structural steel, brick, and northern white ash and cherry woods, are utilized to provide a cost-effective solution. The project was built for US$95 per square foot, less than other recently built churches in the Roman Catholic diocese.

Masonry coursing and technology became essential to the building's aesthetics and functionality. The brick-clad structure conveys a welcoming character appropriate for a place of worship. The curving masonry screen walls at the main entrance reach out to the visitor, symbolizing the outstretched, open arms of the parish community. The entry loggia also blurs the distinction between interior and exterior space. Twelve columns at the front of the building symbolize Christ's apostles. Additional white masonry screen walls articulate secondary entrances and attached chapels.

Inside the building, the two-level marble baptistery serves as an introduction into the main worship space. The fan-shaped eucharistic hall features seating that wraps around the altar platform, thus fostering a sense of community and closeness for the congregation. Two exposed steel trusses support a central light monitor that introduces abundant daylight into the main worship space. As a recall of the church's history, the interior also features stained glass windows relocated from the previous church building. A "Seasons of the Church" tapestry forms the appropriate backdrop for the main altar. The ecclesiastical furniture was designed to complement the architectural design.

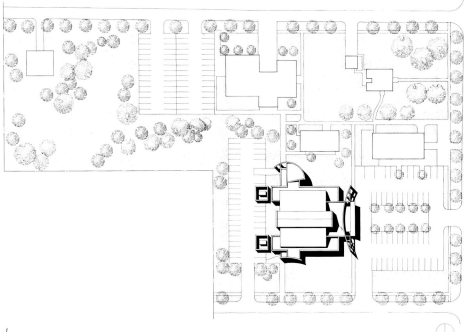

1

2

1 Site plan
2 View of church from northwest
3 Exterior of chapel on church's west side

3

4 Floor plan
5 Baptistery, near entrance to church
6 Interior of chapel, with curved brick wall
7 View on axis from baptistery to sanctuary
Following pages:
   Sanctuary interior is spacious and light-filled
Photography: Jon Miller/Hedrich-Blessing

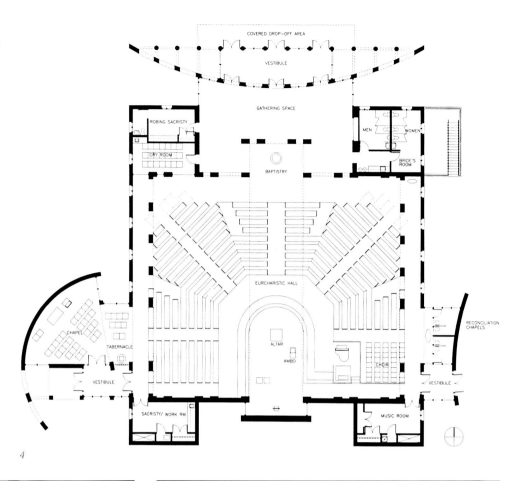

4

5

6

CONGREGATION BETH EL

Hahnfeld Hoffer Stanford Architects

An established, Reformed Jewish congregation in Fort Worth, Texas desired to relocate to a new campus. The congregation wanted far greater emphasis on the internal experience than on the external appearance. Controlled vistas of nature and infusions of natural light were to be incorporated as reminders of God's presence around them.

Taking these factors into consideration and layering them with Jewish history, the architect formed a 47,000-square-foot village of buildings and courtyards, reflecting planning nomenclature of ancient Jerusalem. Incorporating a series of walls with portals, progression through these gateways leads to spaces increasing in sacredness, culminating in the innermost holy of holies—the ark—similar to the procession described for Solomon's Temple.

The campus is divided into four building areas (administration, worship, education, and social) anchored by a commons for informal interaction and gathering. Equally important are the courtyards formed from the spaces between the buildings. Generally walled and gated, the courtyards vary in size and character, providing venues from personal meditation in some to outdoor gathering and play in others.

The sanctuary is designed to seat 600 yet to feel comfortable for groups as small as 200. During high holy days, larger groups are accommodated by an upward folding door separating the chapel from the sanctuary, allowing overflow seating for 750. The chapel seats 150 and is used for smaller gatherings. Both the sanctuary and chapel have views to garden spaces beyond. A Hall of Remembrance enshrines artifacts brought from the former temple. The menorahs on either side of the main entrance gate were relocated from the previous building and set into the new limestone wall.

Desire for timelessness, permanence, and natural materials led to detailing the building in a contemporary yet ancient fashion. Battered sanctuary walls are rendered in large-scale limestone block to recall the Wailing Wall. The vaulted, copper-clad sanctuary roof cants upward to the east and toward Jerusalem. Quartzite flooring was used to recall Jerusalem limestone.

1

2

1 *Detail of east elevation*
2 *View from southeast*
3 *Site plan*
4 *Building welcomes worshippers with extended canopy*
5 *Detail of outdoor garden area*

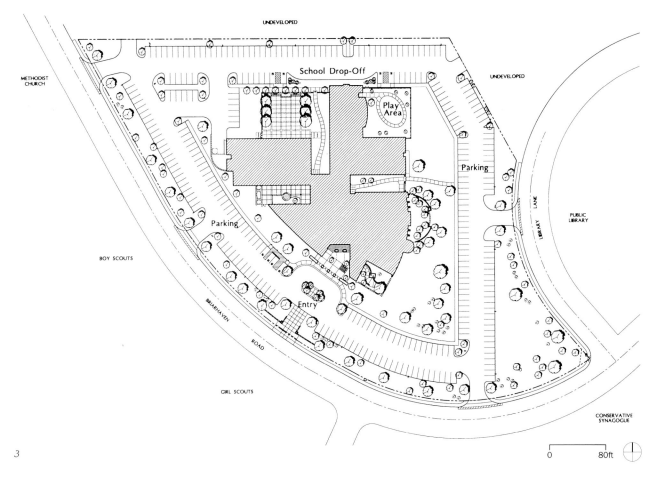

3

4

5

6 Ornamental gates into entry courtyard
7 View from lounge into gathering space
8 Detail of ark doors
9 View of main sanctuary from balcony
Photography: Michael Lyon Photography

6

7

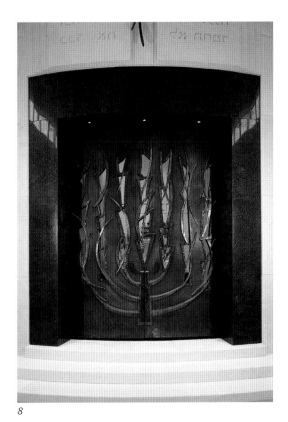

8

9

ST. BONIFACE EPISCOPAL CHURCH

Hammel, Green and Abrahamson

This new church is located on an important rural thoroughfare in the growing suburb of Mequon, Wisconsin. Since the 1950s the parish occupied a small, unassuming worship space placed askew to the rural road it fronted. Having outgrown this worship space, the parish decided to build a new one to accommodate 350 to 400, converting the existing worship space into much-needed classrooms.

A tall and monumental new church faces directly onto Mequon Road, allowing it to develop a civic and urban dialogue with the street. At the hinge point between new and old buildings, a copper spire pins the two compositions together. At the base of the spire is the entrance, with a red door in remembrance of the martyrdom of the saints. The pie-shaped open space is a new gathering space, clad in glass with a view to a woods.

The new worship space features a low and dark base of brick, which is continued inside with heavy burnished concrete masonry and concrete piers. Nestled inside this massive base is a light and airy volume of wood sheathed with copper. The new space is framed in exposed laminated timbers and decking of Douglas fir. The timbers are kept as light as possible through the use of steel tensile rods to produce a truss, with minor compression members turned from wood on a lathe. These trusses are supported on battered cast-in-place concrete piers, placed inside the building enclosure, establishing an inner sacred space with side aisles. A huge clerestory window behind the altar faces due north, allowing a view of the sky including the treetops of a small forest owned by the parish. The wind bracing for this wall forms the timber cross for the worship space.

The church, designed by HGA's James Shields, is clad almost entirely in copper. An altar of two blocks of solid limestone is placed atop a platform of white birch. Pews of cherry on a slate floor are arranged in a combination of antiphonal and basilican seating types.

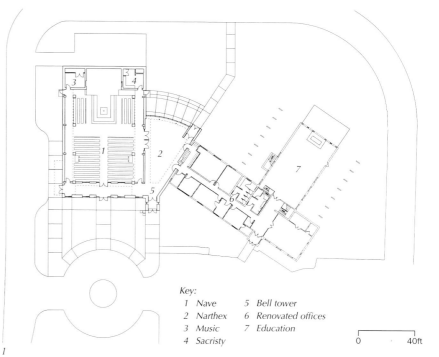

Key:
1 Nave   5 Bell tower
2 Narthex   6 Renovated offices
3 Music   7 Education
4 Sacristy

0   40ft

1

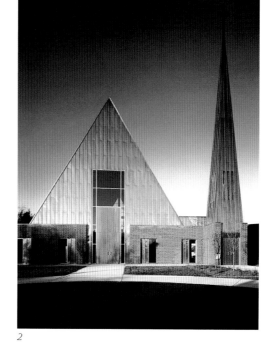

2   3

1 Floor plan
2 Church as it faces the street
3 View of interior from exterior
4 Illumination highlights roof structure
5 Chancel is defined by raised platform
Photography: John J. Korom Photography

4

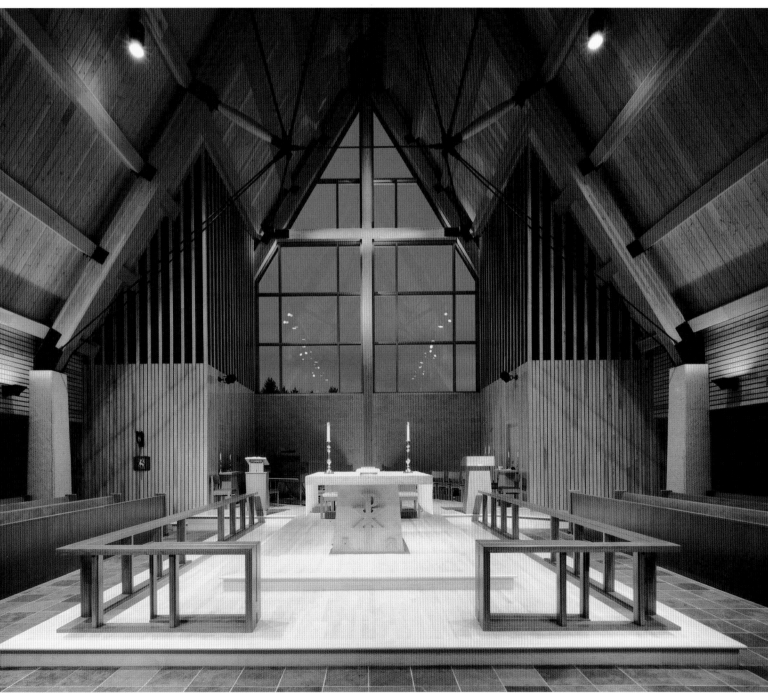

5

St. Mary Magdalen Catholic Church Renovation

Constantine George Pappas AIA

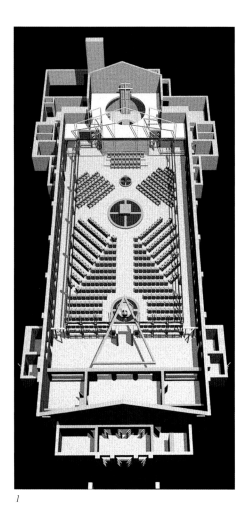

1

St. Mary Magdalen Catholic Church in Hazel Park, Michigan dates from 1955 and had a traditional center aisle with the altar placed at the far end of the church. With seating for 1100 but a diminishing congregation, the parish sought to renovate the church so that it would be more welcoming and comfortable to a smaller community of worshippers. Added were a gathering space, a Blessed Sacrament chapel, and a daily mass chapel. Mark Joseph Costello was the liturgical consultant.

The redesigned interior creates a "church within a church." The new nave, which now seats 450 people, is defined by a suspended aluminum and wood ring. The ring is suspended from the structure above and contains new indirect lighting and a new sound system. Existing structural trusses were painted a light color to reflect the introduction of lighting. Existing windows were replaced to increase natural light levels throughout.

Less seating space allows the introduction of an overflow/gathering space, a Blessed Sacrament chapel, and a new daily mass chapel. Traditional religious fixtures used in the old church were redesigned and introduced back into the renovated space. They include the Stations of the Cross, tabernacle, and central cross. The altar platform, baptismal font, and ambo are centered along the church's axis. Changes to locations of these elements allow the community to gather around the table during mass, touch the holy waters of the font as they enter, and celebrate in the spoken word.

2

1   Plan
2   Seating radiates around new central altar

3

4

5

3 View into sanctuary from overflow/gathering area
4 Baptismal font near sanctuary entry
5 Glazed wall separates overflow/gathering area from sanctuary
Following pages:
    Daily mass chapel at church's east end
Photography: Justin Maconochie/Hedrich Blessing

PILGRIM REST MISSIONARY BAPTIST CHURCH

CCBG Architects

Located only two miles east of the metropolitan cultural center, Pilgrim Rest's new campus in Phoenix, Arizona consists of a 2000-seat sanctuary, community garden, future education and family center, and the existing chapel.

Part of the urban design strategy was to unite the existing chapel with planned program elements and to provide a prominent statement of a progressive sanctuary to the public. The sanctuary is placed on the corner of Jefferson and 14th streets. The community garden is sited between the sanctuary and the existing chapel and future education building to provide a sense of enclosure. A pedestrian connection links the urban fabric through the site, connecting the neighborhood to the west and Eastlake Park to the east.

The architecture juxtaposes the essential character of Protestant Christianity without emphasis upon sectarian tradition and a congregational desire to link the character of Baptist faith with African-American tradition. The portrayal of the rugged character of the Baptist faith is represented in the exposure of structural elements and shapes throughout the project. The African term *Litema* (patterns, relief moldings, engraved patterns representing the play of light and shadow across furrowed fields) is abstracted and united with the structural components to provide compositions that are constantly in flux as the sun describes its daily path. Another African term *Lapa* (courtyard; a place most closely linked with ancestors with a walled perimeter with paths scraped into the floor) is incorporated into the design of the community garden.

The architecture is a sequence of events that culminates at the baptistery and corner tower and cross elements. Canopies guide the pedestrian to three entrance points. Once in the lobby, visitors are reoriented to a diagonal focus on the opposite corner. In the sanctuary, viewers are drawn to the baptistery and central skylight that provides a direct view of the tower and crosses. The circular baptistery rises above the altar and can also be seen from Jefferson Street. The large circular form provides a symbolic gesture to the public of the rituals performed within.

1

2

3

1 Building from the northwest
2 Tubular structure in sanctuary
3 View of sanctuary's floating planes
4 Second floor plan
5 First floor plan
Photography: Courtesy of CCBG Architects

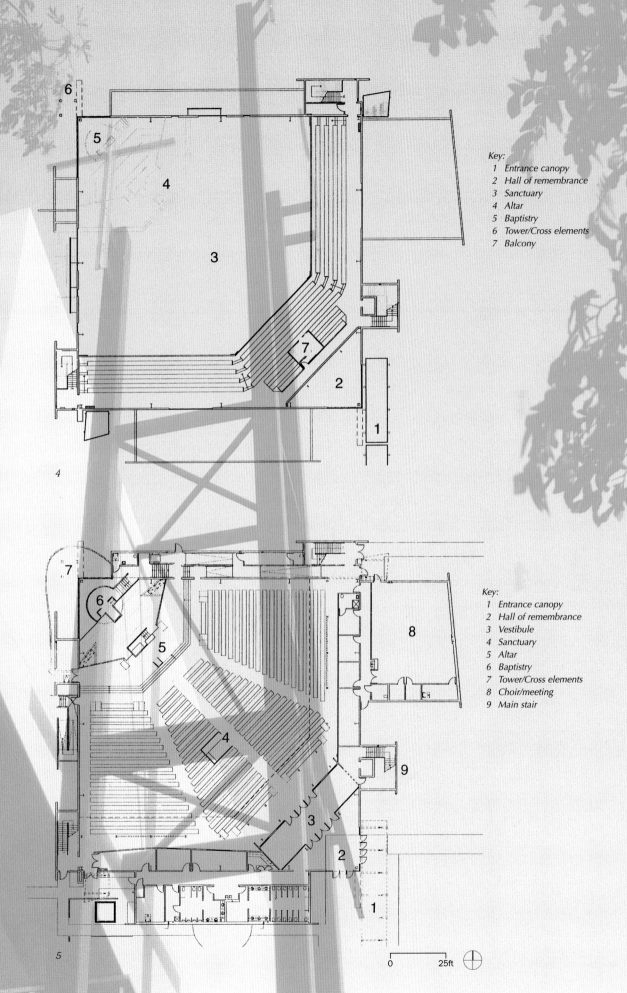

Key:
1 Entrance canopy
2 Hall of remembrance
3 Sanctuary
4 Altar
5 Baptistry
6 Tower/Cross elements
7 Balcony

4

Key:
1 Entrance canopy
2 Hall of remembrance
3 Vestibule
4 Sanctuary
5 Altar
6 Baptistry
7 Tower/Cross elements
8 Choir/meeting
9 Main stair

5

0   25ft

EMANUEL CONGREGATION SANCTUARY RENOVATION

Ross Barney + Jankowski Architects

The design focus of this sanctuary renovation in Chicago, Illinois was a reinterpretation of the sacred space to meet new needs. Because of the decrease in the size of the congregation, and its changing needs and activities, it was determined that the best design response would be one that rested on flexibility and convertibility. The approach by the architect was to use traditional materials and new forms combined with existing artwork to reinforce the significance of the temple.

The form of the new sanctuary-within-sanctuary is based on the transformable nature of the tent. The rear of the existing, auditorium-style sanctuary sloped, and it was determined that this part of the space would be best if converted into a raised platform, which would form the nucleus of the temple interior. Surrounding the platform are translucent panels that are hung between metal poles with stabilizing struts. These fabric structures serve to transform the space, creating a more intimate gathering area within the larger existing sanctuary. When drawn, the panels enclose an intimate sanctuary filled with movable seats, lecterns, and ritual objects that can be grouped in infinite configurations. When open, the panels flank the platform for its use as a stage for social events or for ritual during special worship services.

Overhead, ceiling structures and their supports float above and beyond the platform, lending a sense of the cosmos and its mystery. Its components are light and translucent, and artificial illumination is filtered through the sheer fabric.

1

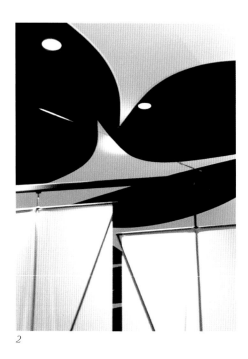

2

3

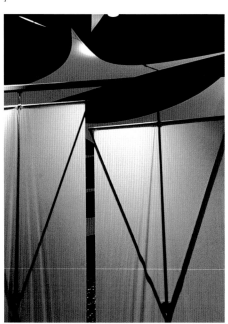

4

5

St. Therese Catholic Church

RDG Schutte Wilscam Birge

St. Therese Parish in Sioux Falls, South Dakota serves a primarily blue-collar, working class community. The site is located on a hill overlooking the city to the west. The 18,000-square-foot building's gathering space frames a direct line to the cathedral within the heart of the city. A beautiful pink quartzite stone is abundant within the soil of Sioux Falls and is used extensively as a building material in older structures downtown.

Two major ideas were explored within the architectural solution—the act of place-making and the notion of duality inherent within St. Therese. Dualism became a recurring theme upon further research of the saint. St. Therese was a cloistered nun who reached the community solely through her religious writings. She was nicknamed "Little Flower" due to her frail body yet fiery spirit and stubborn personality. The rose became her emblem.

The architectural representation of duality manifests itself within the details. Cast-in-place concrete and concrete block are used in concert with wood and steel detailing. This play of concrete mass and the ephemeral lightness of steel and wood embodies dualism. The play of shadows and light reinforces this notion. The cloister canopy at the entry and the *brise soleil* on the west side of the building also tie back to the cloistered nun.

Cast-in-place concrete walls frame views outside, extending the interior space and bringing the landscape into the building. Place-making occurs through concrete walls and columns and local pink quartzite aggregate. The concrete benches on the west elevation act as a datum through which the changing topography is revealed, enabling the building to root itself to its site.

1

2

1   View of church complex from southeast
2   West view of sanctuary wing
3   Altar area as it faces congregation
4   Altar is on axis with sanctuary entry
5   Narthex between sanctuary and classroom wing
6   Detail of altar furniture
7   Filtered daylight in sanctuary
Photography: Tom Kessler Photography

3

4

5

6

7

ST. PETER'S BY THE SEA

Errol Barron/Michael Toups Architects

St. Peter's by the Sea in Gulfport, Mississippi combines a 200-seat Episcopal church and a parish hall in new structures to replace an existing facility built in the 1950s. The site fronts the Gulf of Mexico to the south and a quiet residential street to the north. The site is small but contains several fine oak trees that were saved by careful placement of the buildings. One tree is incorporated into the porch of the parish hall.

The strong regional tradition of the Gulf Coast domestic architecture was an important factor in the design, as were the traditions of Anglican churches inherited from England in the 19th century as part of the American Gothic Revival. The design is an effort to acknowledge these stylistic forces without any literal quotation and to accommodate the needs of a modern parish.

The 13,500-square-foot church and parish hall are linked by porches and a covered walk and are placed to take advantage of the views to the Gulf and to provide a formal entry from the street. The church connects to the street with a curved drive and is set back from the noisy beachfront highway. The parish hall, containing offices, classrooms, and a large fellowship hall is set apart and at a right angle to the church to form a protected court on one side and a chapel garden on the other. There are many fine wood-frame houses along the beach road and the composition is intended to become part of the ensemble through the use of local details and material transformed for the project.

Internally, the church uses an unusual device to combine church and chapel. The reredos of the church forms the back of the chapel and the chapel serves as the choir of the church, providing a hidden source of music for services when needed. The architects designed all the fittings and chandeliers and paid special attention to the acoustical resonance of the church in response to the diverse music programs sponsored by the congregation.

1   Section
2   View of church from the northwest

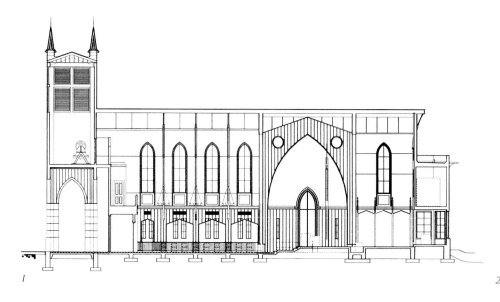

1

3

3 Chapel is found behind raised chancel
4 Floor plan
Opposite:
    View down nave toward chancel
Photography: Alan Karchmer

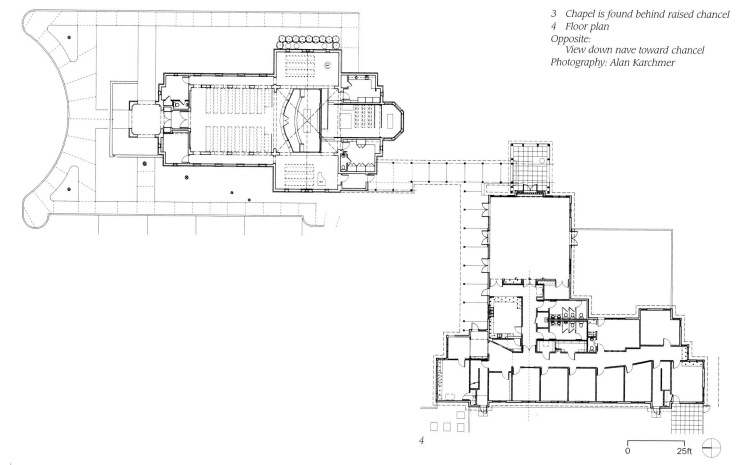

4

0   25ft

5

CONGREGATION B'NAI YISRAEL

Lee H. Skolnick Architecture + Design Partnership

The new synagogue for Congregation B'Nai Yisrael in Armonk, New York marries a respect for nature and the earth with an emphasis on prayer and study. From inside, the natural world remains in view as a constant reminder of the Earth and God's creation. The building takes full advantage of the attributes of its location, while buffering activities from the noise of a nearby road. A low stone wall acts as both a border and a link between the sacred and the secular. As the land slopes away the wall appears to rise and shelter, leading one toward the simple wooden vestibule and the sanctuary beyond.

The open form of the lobby and sanctuary faces the interior of the site, oriented toward the natural landscape and protected from the road by the stone wall and the low block of the school, administrative offices, and social hall. The protected garden is a wonderful place for gatherings, receptions, the building of the sukkah, and other events.

Upon entering through the vestibule, one encounters the lobby space sheltered by a vaulted ceiling, which it shares with the sanctuary. The lobby space is defined by the confluence of the long stone wall, the curved low form of the library, and the wood-paneled wall separating it from the sanctuary. The sanctuary includes specially designed panels that allow the space to be expanded from its normal capacity of 240 to 570 by opening up to the social hall, or 910 by opening out to a tented stone terrace in the garden.

The library shares the lobby with the sanctuary. A skylight centered over the circular portion of the room helps define an area for meetings and informal discussions, or for use of the space as an extra classroom.

A wing of four new large classrooms provides pleasant learning spaces, supplemented by those in the social hall and library. The classrooms are outfitted to utilize the latest in learning technology, while lending themselves to both formal and informal education in a safe, comfortable, and warm atmosphere.

1

2

3

1   Synagogue within the landscape
2   Sanctuary wing as it overlooks outdoor plaza
3   Sanctuary glows at dusk, with ark at center
4   Entry into sanctuary wing
5   Library illuminated from overhead
6   Interior of sanctuary, with view toward ark
Photography: Andrew Garn

4

5

6

SISTERS OF MERCY McAULEY CHAPEL

Constantine George Pappas AIA

This new chapel in Farmington Hills, Michigan represents three powerful geometric forms that also depict the Roman Catholic faith. The chapel is the focal point of the Sisters of Mercy Regional Community of Detroit. The community includes a complex of living spaces, administrative office areas, dining facilities, recreation facilities, an infirmary, and two chapels. The latter serve the needs of daily mass for the sisters. Margaret Bouchez Cavanaugh served as liturgical consultant on the project.

A round, central plan was created to allow one unified space, with the altar table positioned in the middle, equidistant and close to all the participants. Seating capacity totals 125. The intersecting triangular roofs high above the altar and chancel represent the Trinity (Father, Son, and Holy Spirit). As a consequence of the intersecting triangles, a true cross is overlaid onto the plan of the circular chapel.

The placement of the triangles over the altar creates a powerful space that encourages one's eye to look toward the heavens. Low, adjoining roof areas are mysteriously suspended by steel cables. All three images—the circle, the triangle, and the cross—come together to create a juxtaposition of architecture in nature.

Three materials further strengthen the design concept. Brick for the circular portion of the chapel creates a warm, maintenance-free enclosure. Glue-laminated wood members and wood decking in the roof add strength and warmth to the space. Glass openings fill the chapel with natural light and allow participants to spiritually bond with nature.

1   Chapel asserts itself in the landscape
2   View of the round chapel from the north, with existing building at left

3 Floor plan
4 View of roof structure directly above the altar
5 Roof structure becomes a presence when
  illuminated
Photography: Laszlo Regos Photography (1,2,4);
Justin Maconochie/Hedrich Blessing (5)

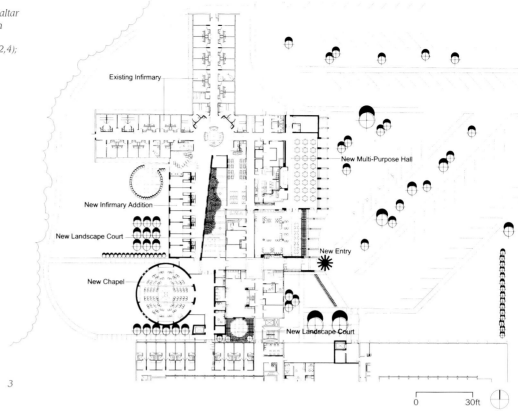

Existing Infirmary

New Multi-Purpose Hall

New Infirmary Addition

New Landscape Court

New Entry

New Chapel

New Landscape Court

3

0   30ft

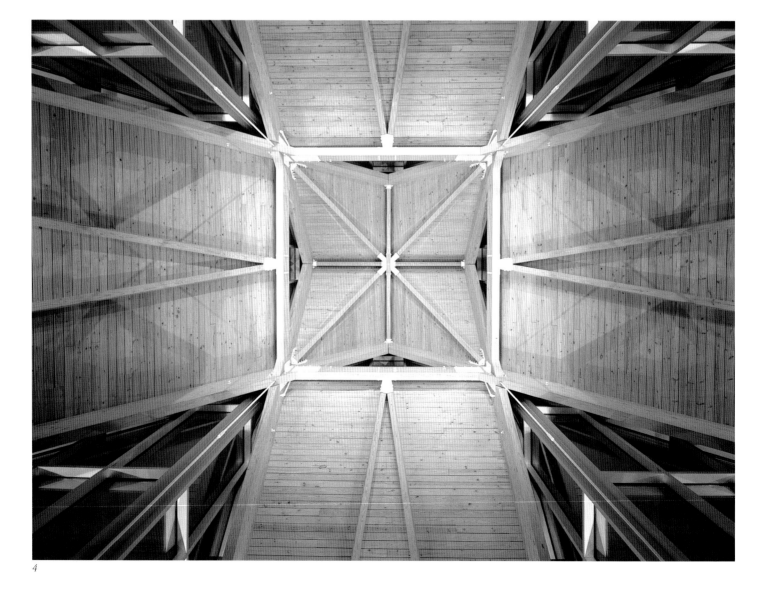

4

5

CHURCH OF CONSCIOUS HARMONY

Lake/Flato Architects

This church complex, built to human scale with honest materials, is well suited to the land upon which it sits and to the practice of the faith of this congregation. The emphasis is on sustainable materials and systems so that the building expresses a reverence for the earth.

The sanctuary, located on a beautiful, natural site in Austin, Texas, is constructed with heavy timber debarked poles, straw bale walls, and wood floors. The round, naturally illuminated space accommodates approximately 375 people. The space is bathed in light from a high lantern, clerestory windows, and vertical slots between the staggered, thick, stucco-finished straw-bale walls. Below the sanctuary is a "kiva" space for more contemplative worship activity.

Classroom buildings circle around a central court with watercourses, a fountain, and a butterfly garden. Insects, attracted to the plants and water, in turn attract birds. Deep porches and long overhangs provide protection from the rain and the hot summer sun. The fellowship hall acts as an open-air breezeway for the courtyard during warm weather and is easily converted to an indoor space with sliding barn doors and radiant heaters during harsh weather.

Car parking is reserved on the uphill side of the property, and footpaths meander through the tree-covered site down to the campus of buildings. All roofs are corrugated metal to assist with clean and efficient harvesting of rainwater that is stored in cisterns and used to irrigate the xeriscaped grounds. Brick pavers are used under the porches and most classroom floors are stained concrete.

1   Church complex's interconnected buildings
2   View of complex as it stretches along the site
3   Walkways shaded by trellis structures
4   Central courtyard of support buildings
5   Site plan
6   Classroom space has exposed roof structure
7   Light in sanctuary is delivered from above
Photography: Hester & Hardaway

1

2

3

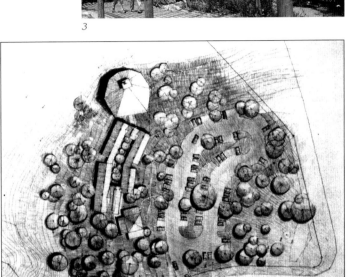

5

4

6

7

ST. JEAN VIANNEY CATHOLIC CHURCH

Trahan Architects

Integrating natural light and the beauty of the surrounding site, utilizing honest, simple materials, and the seamless integration of building systems all weigh heavily in the design of this sacred space. Light and nature are deliberately expressed to engage the senses.

Historically, the Roman Catholic Church has embraced the basilica form, which creates a distinct hierarchy and separation between the seated congregation and the altar platform. Vatican II emphasized the idea of the community gathered around the table in worship. Instead of varying defined spaces and levels of participation, new churches should emphasize the unified body of the church, all participating equally. This revised paradigm for worship, together with the natural wooded site

and a strong desire to integrate nature and natural light into the space, are central in the design of St. Jean Vianney in Baton Rouge, Louisiana.

The sacred place is expressed as a 16,000-square-foot octagon of glass punctuated at the cardinal points by triangular concrete chapels. Communal seating surrounds the altar, which is a raised platform at the center of the space. The choir and presider are all included within this ring of seating, as they come forth from among the people—a true expression of communal worship. Beyond an ambulatory, yet visible to the communal worship space, are three distinct chapels that provide space for private devotional worship. In complement to the gathering concept, eight concrete pillars,

a central oculus, and the vertical layering of architectural elements all result in an overall transcendent experience within the space.

Church doctrine is explicit in stating that simplicity in forms and materials exalts the integrity of worship. The sanctuary is conceived of as a clean, pure space where truth of materials and the expression of building processes further emphasize the sanctuary's spiritual nature. The materials are authentic, pure, and true—without layers, façades, or decoration. Concrete is the natural choice because it is both the interior and exterior finish, has an undeniable sense of stability and permanence, and like the rings of a tree is permanently imprinted with the process of its growth and development.

1

Entry to church, as it faces north
Elevation
Glazed sanctuary glows at night

2

0   20ft

3

4 *View across sanctuary toward Chapel of the Blessed Mother*
5 *Baptismal font, viewed from sanctuary*
6 *Ambulatory surrounds sanctuary along periphery*
7 *Floor plan*
8 *Overview of sanctuary interior*
Photography: Timothy Hursley

4

5

6

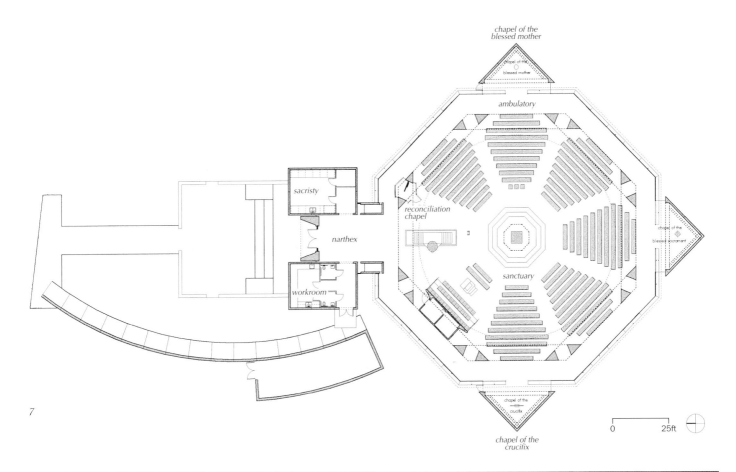

LIVE OAK FRIENDS

Leslie Elkins Architects

This project in Houston, Texas exists due to the faith exhibited by the client, the artist, and the architect. The issue that drove the project from its conception was the housing of a "Skyspace" work donated by artist James Turrell. This piece, a 12-foot-square aperture at the heart of the meeting room, provides an ethereal connection with heaven.

Though Turrell, born a Quaker, had made a similar piece at a school in New York (titled "Meeting"), many in the Houston congregation (which at that time was meeting in a strip-mall dance studio) were unfamiliar with his work. Hiram Butler, a dealer of Turrell's work in Houston, took the artist to a Quaker meeting there. Butler wanted to bring one of Turrell's Skyspaces to Houston, and turned to the local art community to assist in funding the siting of the piece at the new Live Oak Friends Meetinghouse. The church's master plan called for the construction of three buildings; only the meetinghouse has been completed to date, and it has been a true collaborative effort between the congregation and the Houston community at large.

The meetinghouse consists of a pre-function space, the meeting room and a post-function/service area, as well as restrooms. The design includes a 10-foot-deep porch that wraps the building, providing exterior "rooms" for congregating and the possibility for wide overhangs (which shade the interior and assist in maintaining cooler interior temperatures in the inclement Houston heat). Windows and doors can be opened to allow for cross ventilation—assisting in making this building environmentally efficient.

The Skyspace can be viewed by the public every Friday evening, from one hour prior to sunset to one hour after sunset. It has become a place of respite for many as they end the working week, or seek solace and quiet in the city.

1

2

3

1   *Meetinghouse commands its space in the landscape*
2   *Detail of woodwork*
3   *View on axis from entrance to meeting room worship space*
4   *At night, "Skyspace" hovers as a blue field*
5   *Early morning and late afternoon's ethereal glow*
Photography: Ben Thorne

4

5

WHITE CHAPEL

VOA Associates

The White Chapel is a nondenominational place of worship serving the campus of Rose Hulman Institute of Technology in Terre Haute, Indiana. Sited at the western terminus of the larger of two campus lakes, the 5000-square-foot chapel is composed of a wedge-shaped nave supported by a narthex, counseling offices, serving pantry, toilets, and mechanical spaces. The nave is a semi-conical shell defined by a series of steel tube arches, which increase in size from the back of the nave to the front. The exterior of the nave shell is clad in diamond-shaped, stainless-steel panels. The shell is split by a series of vertical ribbon windows and a continuous ridge skylight. The entire east end of the nave is glazed so that the campus creates a backdrop for activities within the chapel.

A long, curved, limestone wall bisects the nave and extends out into the site. Visitors approaching the chapel follow a path along this wall to the entrance. An outdoor garden terrace creates a forecourt to the chapel.

A waterfall and water channel define the southern edge of the terrace, creating a boundary between the everyday world and this place for contemplation and celebration—one that speaks to the spirit as well as the mind.

The essence of the chapel is structure and enclosure, defining the main worship space as a single simple, yet dramatic, volume. As is fitting for an engineering school, the expression of structure and the precision in detailing building systems are the underlying principles of the design. The design seeks to reduce elements of structure and enclosure to their most basic components, eliminating anything that is superfluous or redundant. In this search for elemental simplicity, the geometry of the building drives the design—from the selection of the structural and building enclosure system to the detailing of the mechanical, electrical, and fire protection systems, and the room acoustics. The chapel thus instructs as well as delights.

1   *Exterior of stainless steel shimmers*

1

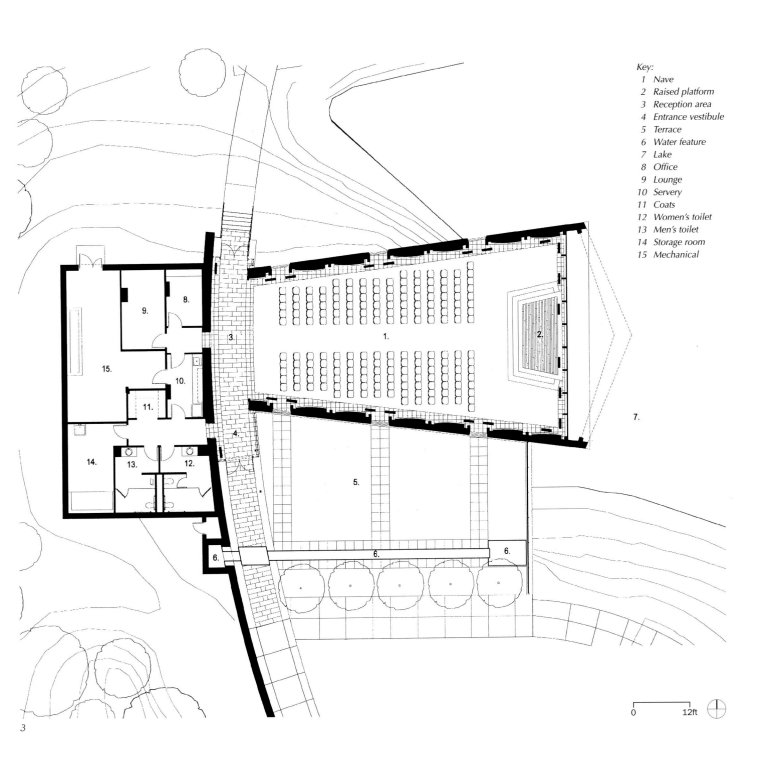

Key:
1   Nave
2   Raised platform
3   Reception area
4   Entrance vestibule
5   Terrace
6   Water feature
7   Lake
8   Office
9   Lounge
10 Servery
11 Coats
12 Women's toilet
13 Men's toilet
14 Storage room
15 Mechanical

0   12ft

3

4   Detail of metal-panel cladding and windows
Opposite:
    Chapel as it faces east

4

AUTHOR AND CONTRIBUTOR NOTES

Dr. Michael J. Crosbie is an internationally recognized author, architect, journalist, critic, and teacher. A former editor of both *Progressive Architecture* and *Architecture*, he is the author of more than a dozen books on architecture, including the first edition of *Architecture for the Gods*, published by The Images Publishing Group in 1999. Dr. Crosbie has written for a number of journals and magazines, including *Historic Preservation*, *Domus*, *Architectural Record*, *Landscape Architecture*, and *ArchitectureWeek*, and has won several journalism awards. He is currently the Editor-in-Chief of *Faith & Form* magazine, the journal of the Interfaith Forum on Religion, Art, and Architecture. He lectures widely on religious architecture and design. Dr. Crosbie is an adjunct professor at Roger Williams University, and has lectured at architecture schools in North America and abroad. He practices with Steven Winter Associates, an architectural research and consulting firm in Norwalk, Connecticut.

For the past decade Dr. John Wesley Cook has been President of the Henry Luce Foundation in New York. Prior to that, he served on the faculty at Yale University for 27 years. At Yale, Dr. Cook administered two graduate programs in interdisciplinary studies and taught the history of art and architecture in the area of religious studies. He has written numerous articles and books on the subject. Since 1985, Dr. Cook has been active in an Asian seminar that studies the religions of Asia and their arts, and he has lectured in India, Thailand, Indonesia, the Philippines, and throughout the US. Dr. Cook is a scholar-contributor to the *Dictionary of Art*, a 37-volume series. In 1996 he was the Deneke lecturer at Lady Margaret Hall, Oxford, England on 20th-century art. In 1998 he was the Hussey lecturer at Oxford, England on sacred art. In the summer of 1999 he was chairman and director of the faculty at the Salzburg Seminar in Austria on "Art, Religion and the Shaping of Culture."

ACKNOWLEDGMENTS

Michael J. Crosbie

Many people were involved in the creation of this book. Thanks are extended to the architects and designers who agreed to have their projects published, and to the clergy and congregations that had the foresight to build them. Special gratitude is expressed to the photographers who generously allowed use of their photographs. Dr. John Wesley Cook's Introduction is an insightful addition to this book for which I am deeply grateful. To my colleagues and friends at *Faith & Form* magazine and the Interfaith Forum on Religion, Art, and Architecture, I express my thanks for suggesting projects, architects, artists, and designers. Finally, I wish to thank Alessina Brooks and Paul Latham of The Images Publishing Group for their support of this publication, and for bringing it to fruition.